Praise for
if you get there before I do...

"Through the pages of this book I saw God's story in and through the lives of David and Ardeth Hoeksema. I marveled at God's mercy and cried at the family's pain and heartache of "letting go" in the emergency room of the hospital that first night and rejoiced at the youth work that David and Ardeth have continued since the death of their 14-year-old daughter. I appreciated David's transparency about his faith and feelings and the commitment David and Ardeth have made to each other while not losing sight of the needs of their teenage son Hans as he grieved. I believe God will use one family's journey through the loss of their daughter and God's faithfulness to help and encourage many others who find themselves unexpectedly experiencing similar tragedy!"

– **Dick Whitworth**, Assistant Vice President for Media,
Northwestern Media, St. Paul, MN

"Every parent's nightmare presented itself to David and Ardeth Hoeksema. They had a choice. They could respond with bitterness, unforgiveness and denial of God. Or, they could honestly struggle through the arduous journey with their faith, forgiveness, and joy in all circumstances. Are you a parent who has "lost" a child through death or their own sinful choices? Are you a person who could encourage such a parent by giving a book filled with hope? Read a testimony of faithfulness. Pass on encouragement to others who are struggling through seemingly impossible grief. *if you get there before I do* is WELL WORTH your investment of time, thought and energy. Learn about the hope of glory which can only come as a result of the birth, life, death and resurrection of the Lord Jesus Christ!"

Dr. Bob Stouffer, Superintendent,
Des Moines Christian School

"The death of a loved one dramatically impacts every aspect of a family from that point forward. At Amanda the Panda Family Grief Center, our focus is to provide a safe haven for children and families to join with their peers as they navigate through their grief journey. The Hoeksema family is a beacon for others who have also had a loved one die. With the turn of each page, David shares the raw, and lasting pain of losing a child. Yet, he also eloquently shares his faith and the blessings that have built into an even stronger bond with God, his family and his community. David noted, "dedicated compassion in action" within the Mercies in Disguise chapter. "You don't ask 'Is there anything I can do for you?' Instead, you just do." Wise, wise words from a man, and his family, who live this every day. The story of Kjrsten's life, cut too short, is an amazing gift and a blessing for all who read *if you get there before I do*."

Charlene "Charlie" Kiesling, Executive Director,
Amanda the Panda Family Grief Center

"Every once in a while, God sends a family through a Season. One such Season that they would never have chosen for themselves. This Season becomes a family's 'God Story'… and that story is intended to be shared. This is such a story."

J. Michael "Mac" McCoy,
Syndicated Christian Talk Show Host,
"The View from a Pew"

"Every one of us will have a life story…but only one. Kjrsten's life story, in our estimation, could have and should have been penned by herself in a writing class. But as a Godly woman, from a Godly family, Kjrsten would have been the first to remind us that 'God is the one who numbers our days.' She fulfilled her life story, albeit so brief, with honor, dignity, compassion and passion. Her father's pen tells the uplifting story, through a tear filled manuscript from a loving father's broken heart, filling most every page. But don't miss the life story of redemption, forgiveness, unconditional love and celebration of a young woman who the author and family WILL INDEED see again as she has arrived before them. Kjrsten lived a life worth reading and adjusting our own stories in the days God gives us breath. Read it. Pass your copy to someone who needs to be reminded of just how short life is and how relationships are the only things that are eternal. And then buy it by the box to give to teachable people around you. You won't be the same after you read this uplifting story. We certainly won't."

Dr. Gary and Barb Rosberg, America's Family Coaches
Co-Authors-6 Secrets to a Lasting Love,
Radio broadcasters & International speakers

"Amazing! This book has the potential to encourage people and draw hurting souls to Christ. Unspeakable loss + unfathomable peace = unbeatable story."

Phil Tuttle, President,
Walk Thru the Bible

MissionHillIowa.com

One family's journey through the loss of their daughter and God's incredible faithfulness

if you get there before I do...

a true story

by David Hoeksema

www.MissionHillIowa.com

Cover and book design by Amanda Marsh/A. Marsh Designs
Front cover photo ©ZoneCreative/iStockphoto. All rights reserved.
Photo gallery designed by Cinnamon Rost/1809 Design

All other interior photos are from the David Hoeksema family collection and are reprinted with permission.

A portion of the profits from the sale of this book is being donated to further missions work around the world.

ISBN: 978-1-4497-7684-8 (sc)
ISBN: 978-1-4497-7685-5 (hc)
ISBN: 978-1-4497-7683-1 (e)

Library of Congress Control Number: 2012922132

WestBow Press books may be ordered through booksellers or by contacting:

WestBow Press
A Division of Thomas Nelson
1663 Liberty Drive
Bloomington, IN 47403
www.westbowpress.com
1-(866) 928-1240

Printed in the United States of America

WestBow Press rev. date: 09/10/2013

DEDICATION

This book is dedicated to my beautiful wife Ardeth.

In my estimation, no one suffered greater or
lost more, than she did. And yet her strength through
this greatest test that life can offer has been an
incredible witness to so many including me.

Ardeth's unflinching faith in Jesus Christ
and her unfailing love for me and our son
will undoubtedly yield a "Well done my good
and faithful servant."

She fought the good fight—she finished the race—
and she kept the faith. (Adapted from 2 Timothy 4:7.)

CONTENTS

FOREWORD

by Collin Raye,
CMA and DOVE award winning singer and songwriter

"No parent should ever have to bury their own child. Death is natural and even expected in families when it happens to grandparents, uncles, aunts, parents and even siblings, once the person has reached a certain age. However, there is nothing natural, or comforting, when we are faced with the death of our precious children. That is simply and powerfully, a tragedy.

As a man who has lost a dear, beloved child of my own, I can attest to the fact that there is no "getting over it". There is no "moving on". You simply live with it.

In my experience, I know there is only one way to survive such a heart crippling loss. That is by and with the Grace of Almighty God, through our Lord Jesus Christ. I know that God can intervene and heal the very sick, or perform miraculous healing of the severely injured at any time He chooses.

However, often times He chooses not to intervene. Only God knows why He chooses His moments of sweet intervention so deliberately. I have come to understand that it is not for us to know why or when He chooses to "step in" and direct those crucial, life altering moments. The truth is He's always there at those moments, front and center. More often than not, He tends to our prayers and petitions of Him in a way that only He understands, with a wisdom and justice far beyond our human comprehension.

"If You Get There Before I Do..." is a beautiful, poetic narrative of God at work in a family who has suffered the ultimate loss of losing a child. It is a heart-warming, yet heart-wrenching story of a precious family following Christ, doing everything right, yet still forced to face the worse scenario a family can be asked to endure.

David Hoeksema is a brilliant writer who weaves the story of their beloved daughter Kjrsten into an absolutely compelling tale of faith, family, love, tragedy, strength, faith, family and finally, faith again. In the midst of a life surrounded in pain and sorrow, their family continued always looking upward in hope and absolute assurance of God being in control.

It is also a "Job" type story. A story of a Christian family's resolve being tested, and of their victory over the powers of darkness who crave that this family simply "give up" and become disgruntled and blame God.

I found their story inspiring and comforting. I believe families who've suffered that ultimate loss of a child, (and I have encountered many of these families since my own sweet child's death), will find comfort and a hopeful security in this book. Furthermore, I believe families who have never had to face such a loss will read this and treasure their precious children more than ever, realizing how fragile and delicate life is, and how fast it can slip away.

Foreword

This is a beautiful, powerful story, written by a wonderful author, that will make you want to hug your children constantly and never let go. You will find strength and hope in the story of a family whom God allowed to suffer massive loss and pain, yet by His precious Grace, have joyfully chosen to praise Him anyway.

Collin Raye

INTRODUCTION

...faith, hope and love. But the greatest of these is love.
1 Corinthians 13:13

December 2012

Naiveté is not necessarily a bad thing. When it came to writing this story, it certainly worked in my favor. Having never published more than a term paper, little did I know what was involved in bringing a story to life.

No one person writes a book, and that is especially true in my case. First and foremost, a great deal of credit must be given to my best friend, Ardeth (who just happens to be my wife of 26 years and counting). Ardeth's encouragement and patient review of each version has been invaluable. We have traveled the journey together, and we are sharing the stories together.

Much credit also goes to our son Hans who was the proverbial 'straw that broke the camel's back' as he cured me of writer's block. Hans began working on a fiction manuscript of his own several months ago that inspired me to quit procrastinating and put pencil to paper and join him in these literary adventures.

Getting the events of our story down on paper was in

many ways one of the most difficult challenges I have ever undertaken. The roller coaster of emotions was intense as I was forced to rehash the pain of so unexpectedly losing our daughter Kjrsten. There were many times when I had to stop typing because I couldn't see the keyboard as I wept unashamedly. But ironically, it was also one of the most satisfying experiences of my life. However, taking the time to remember also brought back memories of the parts I wish I could have forgotten—or had never happened.

This book is for all those who have passed through the deep waters of losing a loved one whose life has been cut short—whether by a premature birth, an unforeseen accident, terminal illness or other unavoidable circumstance.

I can't imagine the levels of despair that people without hope experience in the most painful and trying times of life… broken marriage, cancer, unemployment—and the list could go on and on. As difficult as our unexpected journey "walking through the valley of the shadow of death," I fear that for those without hope, it can become a living death. In 1 Thessalonians 4:13 we are reminded that as Christians we do not "grieve like the rest of mankind, who have no hope."

What happened to our family in the loss of our daughter was a terrible tragedy. But, like the crucifixion of Christ, our story doesn't end in defeat. You'll find that the book speaks of the resurrection—a story of triumph over death—bringing great joy and hope for all who would call on Jesus as Lord of their life.

Hope is largely what sustained us through those darkest days after our daughter Kjrsten's untimely death at the age of 14. And faith is where our hope originates. More than anything, we want others to understand that God loves us, and losing Kjrsten does not change that in the slightest.

As Joni Eareckson Tada, left a quadriplegic in a wheelchair as a teenager in 1967, wisely explained in *The God I Love*, "Sometimes God allows what He hates to accomplish what He loves."

Our greatest desire as you read these stories is that you will clearly see the sovereign hand of God throughout our lives— even in the midst of one of life's greatest challenges—the loss of a child. God loves me, and He loves you too—even when the trials of this life may seek to convince us otherwise.

I say 'stories' because the journey for Ardeth and for me has been more than just Kjrsten's life cut short. It's about forgiveness; it's about healing. It's about grieving and learning to live again. It's about celebrating life with every opportunity we receive so that in the end we can joyously say—we have No Regrets. Ardeth and I have lived this incredible journey for nearly eight years now. For most of this time, I continued to remind myself that our story was in many ways miraculous, and I did not ever want to forget those divine occurrences. As much as I love to tell the story about Kjrsten, a far greater story is what Christ has done for us. That is the story I want to tell.

As you read through the pages of this book, keep in mind that it is not about a tragedy, it is about hope. We know that when we come to the end of our lives here on earth, our daughter will be waiting for us at Heaven's Gate, and we will be reunited with Kjrsten—for all eternity.

Someone once said, "Hope springs eternal." And it does for those who have Jesus and His promise of life eternal—a free gift for all who call on His name.

When God finally convicted me to take pen and paper in hand (or open up my laptop); He also graciously provided the wording. I set out to remember the stories for myself, but as friends and family reviewed each subsequent draft, the encouragement to share these stories with a wider audience emerged. There have been numerous others who have encouraged us along the way. Special thanks to BeInspired Network, Inc., partners Becky Johnston and Scott Brunscheen for their expertise and personal commitment to sharing this story with others.

With much gratitude in my heart,
David

PROLOGUE

Since the spring of 2004, Kjrsten had been experiencing severe headaches. When our local physician examined Kjrsten, one of the first questions she asked, "Have you been taking ibuprofen?" to which Kjrsten replied, 'Yes.'" The physician explained that after a person takes ibuprofen for a while and then stops, the body reacts to the loss by demanding more and thus creating 'rebound' headaches. We went home with this plan—no more ibuprofen. Kjrsten was headache free within five or six days. Problem solved.

Then, the headaches returned. But this time it was much different. Sporadic at first, the headaches had become more frequent and intense over the past few weeks. In fact, Kjrsten had complained of dizzy spells at school recently. So much so, that during one spell she needed to lean against her locker for support. We knew it was time to have her condition evaluated by a specialist. Kjrsten's local physician from Baxter Health Services had recommended consulting a neurologist in Grinnell. "We'll start with some blood and work then have you in for an MRI. We'll start there and see what the neurologist says." She added with emphasis, "We are going to be looking for something else, possibly even a tumor. I just want you to understand."

The weekend came and went uneventfully. A combination of school and church activities kept the entire family hopping. Sunday was just like every other Sunday morning in our house. We headed to church (Sunday school too) as we always did. It was a beautiful day. The sun was shining, and the weather was warm.

Kjrsten knew that on Monday she would be going in for the MRI. And while arranging for the appointment with the neurologist for Wednesday was a simple procedure, it created a considerable amount of angst for Kjrsten. On Sunday afternoon as Ardeth, Kjrsten and I gathered around the center island in our kitchen, we were watching the news. The headline news story featured Terri Schiavo, the 41-year-old brain-damaged woman who became the centerpiece of a national right-to-die initiative, and the ensuing court battle regarding disconnecting her from life support systems.

While watching the coverage and the incredibly personal dilemma Terri's family was facing, Kjrsten began voicing her own concerns about the upcoming appointment with the neurologist. "I know they're looking for a tumor or cancer, and I don't mind admitting that I'm a little scared," Kjrsten shared with us. We reassured her the doctors were being thorough and needed the MRI to eliminate some big issues for the cause of the headaches and dizziness. After the MRI, they would begin looking at other options (definitely an optimistic Ardeth attitude). Kjrsten is a bit more like me, a touch more pessimistic as my wife would say (I would call it a realist).

After some thought and contemplation, Kjrsten said clearly, "I don't want to live my life like that." Then, her beautiful green eyes looked directly into mine, and she said, "Daddy, if anything happens to me, and I'm going to be permanently brain damaged, you pull the plug. You let me go. I'll just get to Heaven before you do." A startling bold statement to which I responded, "Fine, but if you get there before I do, I expect you to be waiting for me at Heaven's Gate when I get there."

And so the deal was struck. We laughed about the whole conversation believing, we'd never have to abide by it.

CHAPTER 1
A FATHER'S LOVE...
NOW AND FOREVER

*See what great love the Father has lavished on us,
that we should be called children of God!*
1 John 3:1

November 30, 1989
Burnsville, Minnesota

After 14 hours of labor, she was finally here—Kjrsten Nicole Hoeksema. Having lived in the suburbs of Minneapolis, Minnesota, since 1986, my wife and I had become accustomed to Scandinavian names and their unique spellings. Not only was our daughter Kjrsten (pronounced keer-sten) destined to go through life spelling her last name for strangers and teachers—she might as well spell the first name too. When it came to choosing a name for our first child, it took us less time to settle on her name than it did for her arrival into this world. A lovely, healthy little girl. At seven pounds, fourteen ounces Kjrsten was perfect—at least in her father's eyes.

Kjrsten was somewhat of a miracle baby. Not in the sense that we couldn't conceive but rather that earlier in our marriage I wasn't sure I wanted children. In fact, I was pretty sure I didn't. My wife Ardeth and I both had busy full-time jobs—and mine was complicated by massive amounts of travel.

As a consultant serving non-profit organizations around the country, it was common for me to be away from home as much as four days a week. Consequently, when I was home, I thoroughly enjoyed spending most of my free time with Ardeth.

In the early years of our marriage, money was very tight, as is the case with most young married couples. A trip to McDonald's to split a 'Big and Tasty' (remember the burger that kept the hot side hot and the cold side cold?) was considered a pretty good date night. Or even better, during the summer months we would splurge and buy specialty popsicles and wander our neighborhood on foot, enjoying the treat and each other's company. As time passed, the budget constraints began to ease, and we started traveling together on vacations. I thoroughly enjoyed the concept of not being tied down. And somehow, the idea of children just didn't fit into my emerging ideal world.

My wife on the other hand was devastated when I shared my concern over an expanded family. She believed, probably because I had told her, that I was all for a family. Left with a burning question of what had changed, she struggled to find peace with this new revelation. After many disagreements and even more tears, Ardeth visited our church in the middle of the week and laid her broken heart at the altar and asked God for His peace. After much prayer and with God's help, she accepted the fact that we might never have children. Ardeth even commented to her mother that she shouldn't count on grandchildren from our side of the family.

As I looked at Kjrsten that cold November morning, I realized how much had changed.

✳✳✳

It was my travel that created what now could only be seen as miraculous intervention. In late June 1988 and while on a flight to New York City, I had the unfortunate luck to sit next to a very talkative fellow business traveler.

During those peak years of travel, I flew so much that every month I would earn a free Frequent Flyer ticket on Northwest Airlines. When you begin recognizing flight attendants—and worse—they remember you, you know you're spending too much time in the air. As a result, I chose to commit most of my air travel time to catching up on my work or my passion for reading. I preferred not to engage in conversation with my fellow road warriors; not from some anti-social behavior but rather to fully utilize the uninterrupted, productive work time.

On this particular flight, that concept was lost on the

passenger seated in 3A (I was in 3B). Now the problem with this configuration is that when party A wants to talk, there is no escape for party B. I was trapped.

As soon as our flight departed from the Minneapolis International Airport, the unintentional intrusions from the passenger buckled into seat 3A began in earnest. The young man was probably in his late twenties—seemingly successful, articulate, and madly in love with his kids. He couldn't help himself. For nearly three hours he talked incessantly about his children—everything from how he couldn't wait to get home to them to how he planned to take his four-year-old son out to dinner and teach the boy how to dine in nicer restaurants. He was nervous about how his son would handle the new adventure and whether the boy would tip over his water glass or knock his silverware off the table. Looking back, I'm sure he was obviously much more nervous about the dining adventure than his son. He shared about how his second child was just learning to talk.

This father loved to share every detail about daily life with his children, and I was forced to listen. After all, he had a captive audience. Where was I supposed to go?

But something changed in me, or at least in my thinking, during that flight. I had never encountered anyone who was so excited about being a dad. To him, it was the greatest opportunity any of us could ever be given. And I finally realized when we landed in New York City that I was missing out. If that young man was representative of what it was like to be a father, then I wanted to experience life the way he was experiencing it.

***

Following a full day of meetings, I finally managed to call Ardeth from the hotel later that evening. We always made it a point even when I was traveling, to make time at the end of the day to visit. The conversations didn't have to be long, but they kept the connection alive between us. Often the phone calls consisted of little more than a quick run-down of each other's day or trivial honey-do lists passed from one to the other.

However, tonight was to be different because I had a startling revelation to share. After concluding the banal chitchat, I shared with Ardeth all about my unofficial traveling companion from the morning flight and his uncontainable exuberance when it came to sharing with a complete stranger about his kids. I informed Ardeth that I had reached a decision —I did want to have children and start a family.

I fully expected a shout of joy and an excited response to my new discovery and proclamation. Imagine my surprise when her only response was, "We'll talk about it when you get home." I think shock had already set in. However, as Ardeth explained to me later, once having gained a peace about not having children, she was not going to rush ahead with excitement and be disappointed should I change my mind again.

But that was the beginning. We didn't talk a lot about starting a family. Maybe it was because it still seemed too fragile of an idea.

Four months later we were celebrating Ardeth's birthday with several friends in our neighbor's home. For her birthday gift, I bought Ardeth a baby rattle with the words 'I love daddy!' displayed upon it. It was my subtle way of letting my wife know that I had not changed my mind. My decision remained firm. When our friends saw the rattle, they asked if we had an announcement to make. We assured them no announcements were in the works yet but that we were ready. And now, 13 months later, Kjrsten was making her arrival.

***

We checked in at Fairview Ridges Hospital in Burnsville on the morning of November 30th after Ardeth's water broke. Unfortunately, she never progressed into full labor. The contractions were sporadic but continued for hours.

Finally, Ardeth was given a spinal block to help with the pain. I remember watching Ardeth as she sat on the bed waiting for the physician to perform the procedure. I had never felt so helpless in all my life. Seeing Ardeth in such pain and not being able to aide her was frustrating and heartbreaking at the same time. The nurse instructed Ardeth to remain very still to ensure they wouldn't need to repeat the procedure. So, Ardeth quietly rested her head on the nurse's shoulder, and when the contraction came, she remained motionless. Thankfully, the procedure had to be performed only once.

Additionally, a fetal monitor was attached to the baby in utero in order to better monitor her vitals during the long hours of labor. Shortly following the spinal block, the nurse came rushing back into the delivery room, announcing the baby was in distress. A warning on the fetal monitor indicated the baby's heart rate had dropped to an alarming rate. I just stood in a corner of the hospital room while the attending physician and three nurses rushed around tending to Ardeth. Now I was becoming alarmed and could not stop the tears as I began to cry. The attendants repositioned the bed so Ardeth's head was down and placed an oxygen mask on her face. At that moment Ardeth raised her head, mask and all, and looked at me as I stood quietly weeping in the corner. She silently mouthed the words to me, "It's okay, I'm fine."

A long 15 minutes later, the birth team was satisfied that the baby was once again stable and quietly left the room. It was all I could do to catch my breath. I slowly knelt by the bed and softly told Ardeth, "I don't know this baby, but I know you. I can't lose you. So if it comes to a choice, I choose you."

Nearly four hours later, and after we'd played multiple hands of cribbage, little progress had been made in bringing the baby into the world naturally. It was finally decided that Ardeth and this child needed some help. It was obvious that a cesarean was the only remaining option. They wheeled my wife into surgery with me—a young expectant father suited up in blue scrubs—trailing behind. By this time I was calm and relaxed because Ardeth and baby seemed fine.

✳✳✳

As the son of a pastor and missionary, I ultimately spent most of my formative years attending school in rural Hardin County, Iowa (named in honor of Col. John J. Hardin, of Illinois, who was killed in the Mexican-American War). Consequently, working on the local farms while attending New Providence High School had provided quite an education, including witnessing more than one surgery on pregnant farm animals in distress.

In the operating room the hospital staff politely positioned a chair near Ardeth's head for me to use while observing the surgery. I quickly abandoned that offer for a better view of the action. After waiting in the hospital for 14 hours, the delirium had begun to set in. That explained why I must have felt the need to comment on the operation to the surgeon who was working intently to bring our baby into this world. I said, "The last time I saw a cesarean was on a sow" to which the surgeon never missed a beat in his reply, "Well, let's hope we don't have a litter of 10." He must've been from farm country too. Thankfully, Ardeth laughed as well.

Several hours after midnight, mother and baby were fine. And it was time for me to go home, grab a quick nap and shower, with plans to return to the hospital later that morning.

***

Driving away from the hospital in the wee hours of that cold November morning, I reflected on what had just happened. I was a father. Looking at Kjrsten for the first time, I knew that God was an awesome God and that babies are His greatest miracle. And to think at one time in the not so distant past, I was convinced I didn't want children.

As I made my way west on County Road 42, I was suddenly struck with a premonition. I heard a voice inside me saying, "David, someday you will have to give her away." And the tears began to flow down my cheeks, obscuring my vision and complicating the drive home. I hardly knew this new bundle of joy, and the thought of giving her away to some other man, even in the distant future, was heartbreaking.

It wasn't until nearly 15 years later that the true meaning behind those words became clear.

CHAPTER 2

SUNSHINE AND SHADOW

"For I know the plans I have for you,"
declares the Lord, "plans to prosper you and not to harm you,
plans to give you hope and a future."
Jeremiah 29:11

1989 – 2004
Minnesota and Iowa

As my wife Ardeth and I celebrated our first Christmas with our newborn daughter, Kjrsten Nicole, I was reminded of how quickly our lives can change. We suddenly found ourselves facing the joys and challenges of first-time parenthood. Looking down at this small miracle sleeping peacefully in my arms, I realized how much God had been present in all the circumstances leading to this moment.

Our trek to Minnesota had been an adventure in itself. I joined Growth Design Corporation, a consulting company based in Milwaukee, Wisconsin, fresh out of college. I had graduated from William Penn University in Oskaloosa, Iowa, in 1983, majoring in history with minors in Computer Science and Industrial Arts. Rushing through my bachelor's degree program, I was able to graduate in two years instead of the usual four by taking summer courses and winter break

(J term) credits as well. I had been accepted for the fall term at Drake University's School of Law in Des Moines, Iowa, and was contentedly working during the summer months.

Unexpectedly, I received a phone call from Byron Tweeten, then president of Growth Design Corporation. While serving as president of the student council at William Penn, I had the opportunity to accompany the university president, John Waggoner, on frequent alumni fund-raising events and had met Byron on several occasions.

Byron got right to the point. "Dave, I have a job for you. Are you interested?" At the time, I really wasn't but was intrigued with the idea of the 'big city' and of saving some additional money for law school. So I ventured to Milwaukee, met the rest of the Growth Design team, and ultimately accepted a position paying $12,000 a year—not realizing just how little that compensation was (even by 1983 standards).

Despite the low entry pay, Growth Design was a wonderful experience, and my tenure there proved to be a great apprenticeship that ultimately paved the way for me to consult independently later in life. As a result, I never did enroll in law school. Instead, I spent the next six and a half years working for Byron at Growth Design, surrounded by truly gifted professionals while assigned to various cities to work—first in Des Moines, then Milwaukee, and ultimately the Twin Cities. And, it was here in Burnsville, a suburb of Minneapolis that we were blessed with the birth of our first child, Kjrsten on November 30, 1989.

***

Life changes quickly. After the birth of our daughter Kjrsten, my wife Ardeth and I were blessed 22 months later with a son we named Hans (again in the Scandinavian tradition).

Because I traveled so much on business, even as a weary road warrior, I made a concerted effort to ensure that the kids were my priority when I was at home. Off the road, one of my favorite early morning family activities was to take the kids out for breakfast prior to dropping them off at school.

On one memorable Friday morning Kjrsten, Hans and I got up early so we could run into New Prague for breakfast at the Fish Tail Grill. Ardeth was heading to our church where she served part-time in the office. After a meal filled with laughter, I decided that the thought of spending the day hanging out at Camp Snoopy in the Mall of America was a much better idea than dropping the kids off at school. So I called Ardeth at the church office and handed my cell phone to my four-year-old son Hans. He very directly explained to his mom that, "Dad is teaching us a new game today. It's called playing hookey." However, dad was too big of a chicken to call the school office with the news that the kids wouldn't be coming in—and not due to illness. Thank goodness for moms!

Even when the kids were at a young age, we began to instill the values and ethics we believed were important for their lives down the road. While Hans was still quite young, I was impressed by reading the book, *Raising a Modern-day Knight* by Robert Lewis. It clearly emphasized how important it was for us, as fathers, to take an active role in mentoring our sons to become the gallant and chivalrous men the next generation so desperately needs.

We began with basics, as simple as holding a door open for a lady; giving up your seat in a crowded waiting room to a lady; and never, under any circumstances, hitting a lady. So there he was, all of four years old, and when we'd approach a door to a restaurant or the mall, Hans would run ahead and get the door for his mom. Often, the door was so heavy the little kid struggled to pull it open. On one particular occasion as we arrived at the door, Hans had forgotten his role. Ardeth patiently stood quietly at the door and waited. Almost immediately, Hans thumped his forehead with the heel of his hand, rushed around his mom, and tugged the door open. "Sorry, Mom. I forgot," he apologized. But the lessons took hold, and we were pleased to see Hans rushing to open doors for strangers as well. Many times strangers would compliment us on the manners of our polite and well-behaved children.

However, grasping the 'never hit a lady' rule was more difficult for Hans to comprehend and abide by. After an argument with his sister, Hans exclaimed, "Dad, it's not fair. She hits me. Why can't I hit her back?" I simply shrugged my shoulders and agreed with him, "You're right, Hans. It's not fair. But that's the way it is."

It was just as important for me to model for Kjrsten what she should expect from future men in her life. Beginning with her tenth birthday, Kjrsten and I would celebrate with a 'daddy date night.' I'd put on a suit and tie, and with Kjrsten wearing a beautiful dress, we'd go to a fine dining restaurant for dinner. For the entire evening, I made sure I opened the car door for Kjrsten, helped her with her coat, and pulled out her chair at the table. As I modeled for my daughter all the kind gestures that were appropriate and should be expected from

14

her future suitors, I informed her, "If a young man ever drives to our house to pick you up for a date and honks the horn waiting for you to come out—he's history. Wave him off and send him on his way."

After several years, we made the difficult decision to leave Minnesota and return to my roots in Iowa. One of the greatest challenges in leaving Minnesota was saying good bye to the wonderful youth from our Sunday school class. We began as their teachers when they were in the eighth grade and continued with them for the next three years. Before we left, we met at our country home and shared communion together. Our little farm had been host to tomato fights, pool parties, controlled prairie burns, formal dinner nights for them and their dates and all kinds of other festivities together. Years later we were privileged to attend their high school graduation parties and even their weddings at a later date.

(To get a glimpse of the family in their early years, see Afterword: Answering the Call.)

✳✳✳

In October of 2000, we relocated to Iowa to be closer to my family. When we moved to Baxter, we bought 120 acres of timbered pasture and rolling crop ground to start our new life in farm country. For us, it was our own modern version of *Little House on the Prairie.* Our first priority was to build our new home. And I do mean 'build it'—from the ground up. Since Ardeth and I had worked side by side on constructing our previous home in Northfield, Minnesota, we decided to tackle this one together as well. Acting as our own general contractor, we recruited each of the sub contractors along the way. We framed the house ourselves and enlisted the help of my three older brothers when necessary to help set roof trusses and other heavy aspects of the project. The house took 14 months to complete, but we were thrilled with the end result. Our family of four moved into our ranch home, overlooking a good-sized pond in December of 2001. Almost daily I would find myself looking contentedly out our front windows with my gaze coming to rest on the sun-dappled pond and give thanks for my "little bit of Heaven" here on earth.

Over the next several years, our little family was incredibly blessed. Nary a day went by that Ardeth and I didn't consciously thank God for how He had richly provided for us. My consulting business was doing well, and our children were blossoming into youth with strong faith convictions of their own. I remember saying on more than one occasion that "I could die a happy man knowing both of my children know the Lord—and that we'll meet again in Heaven."

✳✳✳

Visiting the country is easy. Living in the country requires a great deal of work. There are always more projects to be done than time to do them, but we tackled them together. As a team of four, we cut down trees and cleared multi-floral rose in order to build a cabin overlooking the two-acre pond. We stocked it with largemouth bass and blue gill and spent many a summer evening waiting for the 'big ones' to bite.

Sometimes, we'd take our little row boat out into the

middle of the pond and drop anchor while Hans and Kjrsten used it as their swim platform.

One of our favorite summer activities was to sit on the long covered front porch of our home and watch for the storms as they rolled in from the west across Clear Creek. We'd listen for the thunder and see the lightening striking at the bottom of the hill as the storm climbed upwards and through the cornfield to the edge of our yard. We were relieved as it rumbled noisily over the top of our house without leaving any damage as it continued its steady march to the east.

Little did we know what kind of storm was brewing for our perfect little family.

CHAPTER 3

STORM CLOUDS GATHERING

Therefore do not worry about tomorrow, for tomorrow will worry
about itself. Each day has enough trouble of its own.
Matthew 6:34

September 10–15, 2004
Baxter, Iowa

Life changes quickly. Our little family of four was growing up fast. Hans was loving 7th grade and full contact football. Kjrsten on the other hand was now in 9th grade and blossoming into a confident young woman.

She inherited her mother's beautiful hair—luxurious strawberry blonde falling nearly to her waist. With bright and expressive green eyes (also a gift from her mother) Kjrsten's only complaint was her nose (a gift from her father); always feeling it was too big for her face. But even now as she had matured, her face had caught up with her nose, and she had grown into a lovely girl with a well-proportioned face.

Kjrsten was a fighter, stubborn and strong. I remember one particular summer day, Hans, Kjrsten and I were working outside the barn, constructing a sorting corral for the calves. It was a hot, sticky day and the work was not progressing as well as their father would have liked. I commented to both my children that if "their attitudes and productivity didn't improve, we'd be out here all day." I heard Kjrsten mutter a reply under her breath. I challenged her by asking what she had muttered. Kjrsten simply replied, "Then I guess we'll be out here all day." With her simple, direct and honest reply, it was all I could do to stifle a fit of laughter.

The kids worked hard at raising cattle which proved to be a multi-faceted positive experience. Not only did it allow the kids to earn money for college, it also taught them many more practical life lessons. I took them to the local bank in Baxter where they opened a checking account. Then, I helped them work with the loan officer to secure a loan to purchase the calves and buy feed throughout the year. When the next fall came around, it was time to load the fattened cows and take them to Tama to the livestock auction. And it was back to the bank to settle the loan.

Life is a gamble. Sometimes the market was high, and they made good money. At other times, they weren't quite so fortunate. But whatever the end result, they both took their share of the proceeds, set aside 10 percent for tithe to the church, kept 10 percent for fun money and saved the rest.

***

Kjrsten excelled at everything she set her mind to. A straight 'A' student, a starter on the freshman volleyball squad and one of Dad's right hands on the little farm we called a hobby. Kjrsten loved the outdoors. As a family, we spent a great deal of time working together fixing fence, baling hay, riding four wheelers, and feeding the cows and chickens and horses and dogs and cats. She loved animals and always dreamed of marrying a farmer and settling into our house in the country forever.

This particular week, Kjrsten's journal entry for a school assignment was entitled: 'Someone I Admire.' As it turned out, she wrote about me. Not surprising since Kjrsten was like me in many respects. In many ways that could be good—in other ways, not so much. Her journal entry read like this:

Someone that I admire or look up to as a great person is my dad. I look up to my dad. The reasons I admire him are that he is very simple and straightforward. He doesn't care what other people think about him. He doesn't beat around the bush. He tells exactly what he thinks and doesn't apologize for it. My dad is also a very strong Christian, which I also admire. I hope to be just like him someday. My dad is a hard worker and he is the person I want to be just like. He won't change or put on airs to impress people. He is who he is and is proud of it. I wanna be that too.

—Kjrsten Hoeksema, high school freshman, 2004

***

Since the spring of 2004, Kjrsten had been experiencing severe headaches. When our local physician examined Kjrsten, one of the first questions she asked, "Have you been taking ibuprofen?" to which Kjrsten replied, 'Yes.'" The physician explained that after a person takes ibuprofen for a while and then stops, the body reacts to the loss by demanding more and thus creating 'rebound' headaches. We went home with this plan—no more ibuprofen. Kjrsten was headache free within five or six days. Problem solved.

Then, the headaches returned. But this time it was much different. Sporadic at first, the headaches had become more frequent and intense over the past few weeks. In fact, Kjrsten had complained of dizzy spells at school recently. So much so, that during one spell she needed to lean against her locker for support. We knew it was time to have her condition evaluated by a specialist. Kjrsten's local physician from Baxter Health Services had recommended consulting a neurologist in Grinnell. "We'll start with some blood work then have you in for an MRI. We'll start there and see what the neurologist says." She added with emphasis, "We are going to be looking for something else, possibly even a tumor. I just want you to understand."

The tests were scheduled for blood work-up on Friday, September 10th; an MRI on Monday, the 13th and the consultation would be with the neurologist on Wednesday, the 15th.

Life went on as usual. Kjrsten and Ardeth went to the freshman football game at Colfax-Mingo on Thursday night. Kjrsten enjoyed hanging out with her friends while they cheered for their classmates on the team.

On Friday morning September 10th, I took Kjrsten to the hospital for her blood tests in advance of the MRI scheduled for the following Monday. While at the hospital, we ran into Travis Ethridge, a freshman who had injured his ankle at the ninth grade football game the night before and who was just now leaving the hospital on crutches. Some good-natured ribbing between the two freshman classmates ensued.

Later that evening, our family went to the varsity football

game. Driving away from the parking lot, Ardeth, Kjrsten and her friend Megan Stratton even managed a Chinese fire-drill after the game at the main intersection in our small rural Iowa town. Life felt pretty good.

***

The weekend came and went uneventfully. A combination of school and church activities kept the entire family hopping. Saturday included a North Polk volleyball tournament in Alleman. Kjrsten rode the bus over with the team while Ardeth drove to the tournament. Hans and I had projects around the farm to finish up, so we joined them later in the day.

Following the tournament, Ardeth and Kjrsten headed to Ankeny to shop because that is apparently what women do. Those were special times for mother and daughter to be together.

And Sunday was just like every other Sunday morning in our house. We headed to church (Sunday school too) as we always did. It was a beautiful day. The sun was shining, and the weather was warm.

Kjrsten knew that on Monday she would be going in for the MRI. And while arranging for the appointment with the neurologist for Wednesday was a simple procedure, it created a considerable amount of angst for Kjrsten. On Sunday afternoon as Ardeth, Kjrsten and I gathered around the center island in our kitchen, we were watching the news. The headline news story featured Terri Schiavo, the 41-year-old brain-damaged woman who became the centerpiece of a national right-to-die initiative, and the ensuing court battle regarding disconnecting her from life support systems.

While watching the coverage and the incredibly personal dilemma Terri's family was facing, Kjrsten began voicing her own concerns about the upcoming appointment with the neurologist. "I know they're looking for a tumor or cancer, and I don't mind admitting that I'm a little scared," Kjrsten shared with us. We reassured her the doctors were just being thorough and needed the MRI to eliminate some big issues for the cause of the headaches and dizziness. After the MRI, they would begin looking at other options (definitely an optimistic Ardeth attitude). Kjrsten is a bit more like me, a touch more pessimistic as my wife would say (I would call it being a realist).

After some thought and contemplation, Kjrsten said clearly, "I don't want to live my life like that." Then, her beautiful green eyes looked directly into mine, and she said, "Daddy, if anything happens to me, and I'm going to be permanently brain damaged, you pull the plug. You let me go. I'll just get to Heaven before you do." A startling bold statement to which I responded, "Fine, but if you get there before I do, I expect you to be waiting for me at Heaven's Gate when I get there."

And so the deal was struck. We laughed about the whole conversation, believing we'd never have to abide by it.

✳✳✳

From an early age Kjrsten bravely faced physical challenges. State-required vision screening at her Montessori pre-school in 1995 revealed the condition in which the brain tells the eye to stop working—amblyopia, or "lazy eye." Despite numerous episodes of patching over the years, Kjrsten Kjrsten was legally blind in her left eye and required verification from her optometrist that the right eye fully be compensated before she could get her driver's license permit.

The next day on Monday, September 13th I drove Kjrsten to the Newton Hospital for the MRI procedure. Two days later, Ardeth took the day off work to pick up the x-rays at the hospital. After a short drive back to Baxter to pull Kjrsten out of school, they were off to meet with the neurologist at his office in Grinnell to review the results. Ardeth and Kjrsten watched as he pulled the x-rays from the large manila envelope and placed them on the lighted screen to study them. After several seconds of seemingly contemplative analysis, he announced "I've never seen that before." Hardly the words we were hoping to hear.

The neurologist proceeded to describe what he was seeing in the MRI images. There was a void in the left lobe of her brain approximately the size of a quarter. Ardeth asked him, "What could have caused the void?"

"I would imagine that what we are seeing is the result of Kjrsten suffering a stroke while she was still in the womb," was his explanation. After much questioning, the neurologist concluded the void was not causing the headaches, and we'd have to keep testing.

What a blessing for all of us that there wasn't a tumor or cancer involved. While we may not have known what was causing the headaches, we knew what wasn't.

He did observe that her sinuses were full and prescribed an antibiotic for Kjrsten to begin treatment. Unfortunately for

Kjrsten, a side effect cautioned that the medication 'could stunt growth.' At only five feet tall, Kjrsten admonished Ardeth, "to fully investigate the side effects because if there is any chance I could still pick up an inch or two of height, I want them."

✳✳✳

As they left the neurologist's office, Kjrsten was greatly relieved and in high spirits. This straight A student whimsically teased Ardeth, "Just think what I could have been with a whole brain!" It was definitely a time for celebration. They concluded that a stop at Subway, their favorite sandwich shop was in order, before heading back to school. Savoring the news and their friendship, Ardeth and Kjrsten enjoyed what was to be one of their last mother-daughter moments together.

That Wednesday evening was full of activity focused on science class projects. Kjrsten was concerned over a report and presentation that was due on Friday. So, while Ardeth was delegated to reviewing the presentation materials, I worked with Kjrsten on her speech. We made plans to finish it together the following evening, after her volleyball match, taking place in Alleman again.

CHAPTER 4

THE BEST OF TIMES...
THE WORST OF TIMES

"So do not fear, for I am with you; do not be dismayed,
for I am your God. I will strengthen you and help you; I will
uphold you with my righteous right hand. "
Isaiah 41:10

September 16, 2004
Ogden, Iowa

It was a beautiful autumn morning, and the day was full of promise. I always enjoyed seeing the early morning sun reflecting off the pond with its golden hues bathing the changing colors of autumn in the trees surrounding our little piece of Heaven. We had truly been blessed, and I never took it for granted. When we relocated to Iowa, we worked day and night for months—from running a business to building our home on land reclaimed from Iowa soybean fields to raising a family. I would look out our front window and comment, "Right here is where I want to spend my remaining years."

Hans was preparing for his first seventh grade football game of the season in Ogden, and after the previous Saturday's tournament, Kjrsten was set for another volleyball match against the North Polk school district, located in Alleman. Not unusual for families with kids involved in school activities, breakfast was a quick affair in our house with everyone running in different directions. I was preparing to take Hans for an early morning orthodontist appointment 25 miles away in Ankeny.

Before leaving for the orthodontist appointment that morning, I called downstairs to Kjrsten in her basement bedroom to tell her good bye. Kjrsten trotted up the stairs with her wet hair piled on top of her head, wrapped in a towel. As I stood at the top of the stairs, Kjrsten ran up the stairs and, stopping two steps below where I stood waiting, bid me a cheery goodbye with a huge smile and tipped her head back, accepting a kiss on the forehead while holding the bundle of waist-long hair in a towel with both hands.

Off I went with plans to meet my wife later and pick up my parents who wanted to join us for Hans' football game. It was a difficult choice since both his game and Kjrsten's volleyball match were scheduled simultaneously. Figuring that the junior high football schedule consisted of only five games and the volleyball team had nearly 20 remaining games, we opted to cheer for the football team on this Thursday afternoon.

After Hans and I drove away heading to Ankeny, Ardeth helped Kjrsten gather her volleyball gear for that afternoon's game while Kjrsten confirmed what she needed for her science presentation on Friday. With last minute goodbyes, they both left in different directions—one to school and one to work— but parting with the promise of reuniting at home later that evening to finish the science project.

Thanks to her school permit, Kjrsten drove off for school in the Oldsmobile 88 hand-me-down. She had learned to drive behind the wheel of our ancient Ford F-150 pickup truck when she was just 8 years old. I recall fondly of the time, while living in Northfield, Minnesota, we had 40 acres of rolling pasture and hay ground. Kjrsten loved animals even then, especially an ancient horse nearly 30 years old named Buffy. We needed hay for Buffy and Freckles (another old-timer) and for the calves that she and her brother raised. We contracted in shares with our neighbor to put up the hay. He would bale it, take his cut in large rounds and we took ours in regular square bales. It always seemed as though I was traveling on business when our neighbor Jeff Dokken was ready to bale. Consequently, often times our bales were left on the ground for us to pick up later and stack in the barn.

One summer day, Ardeth came home from working part time at the church to discover all the recently baled square hay bales out of the field and neatly stacked in the barn. "How did you get that done all by yourself?" she asked me. "I had a little help," I said. Ardeth's ESP kicked into overdrive, "How did you do it?" she asked again. "I let Kjrsten drive, and I loaded the hay bales. It worked really well," I assured her. I purposely failed to mention that since Kjrsten was too short to reach the pedals in the truck, she pulled herself forward with the steering wheel and hung on for dear life. Now at 14, she had her school permit which allowed her to drive to and from school and school events. And at only five feet tall, Kjrsten's feet still just barely reached the pedals.

Sometimes Kjrsten's zeal and exuberance could outweigh her better judgment. Earlier that spring, our cows had gotten out of the pasture and were heading into the soon to be planted bean field. As I shouted out instructions to head them off, Kjrsten hopped behind the wheel of my Ford Taurus sedan and tore off down the gravel driveway, across the dam of our pond, and proceeded to turn right—directly into the field to cut off the escaping bovines. When we finally corralled the cows and arrived back home, the Taurus was covered in mud and had dried corn stalks sticking out from the fenders. I later commended Kjrsten's quick decision-making but questioned if the pick-up truck might have been better suited to the quick cow roundup.

***

September 16th proved to be a perfect afternoon for football. Hans had been playing football since we moved back to Iowa in 2000. Faced with the dilemma of most Iowa schools not having a hockey program like those in Minnesota, Hans was unsure of a suitable alternative. When I suggested football to him at the tender age of ten, he responded gravely, "You could get hurt playing football." I asked him, "Would you rather get tackled on the grass or on the ice?" All of a sudden, football didn't seem quite so daunting.

This first football game of the season was a big event. My parents, Marvin and Doris, rode with us to the game. Grandma and Grandpa Hoeksema were big fans and I don't mean just of football.

During the fifteen years we lived in Minnesota, they always made Hans and Kjrsten priorities in their lives—frequently making the trip from Iowa to Northfield to visit our family for the weekend. Even in our regular long-distance phone calls, they always enjoyed visiting with the grandkids—

sometimes I think more than they wanted to catch up with me or Ardeth.

Kickoff for the eighth grade game was at 4:30 pm, and for junior high, regulations call for each quarter to be 10 minutes instead of the 15-minute quarters for varsity. With the eighth grade game running long, the seventh graders waited until nearly 5:45 pm for the start of their game. Hans played center—not the largest of the offensive lineman but quick enough to block for his team on the field. The only part that bothered him was the shotgun snap. "I hate it when they call a play out of the shotgun," he would lament. "There's nothing quite like seeing the hiked football sail over the quarterback's head and you with nowhere to hide from the eyes of the crowd."

Ardeth and I were sitting in the stands near the father of Hans' classmate whose wife was attending the volleyball match where Kjrsten was playing. Jeff and Deb Dillon have two children the same age as our two were at the time—Mark who played football with Hans and Haley who played volleyball with Kjrsten.

Near the end of the eighth grade game, Deb Dillon called her husband Jeff on his cell phone to let him know that the ninth grade volleyball match had finished early, and their daughter Haley was riding home with her instead of waiting around to ride on the school bus since the junior varsity and varsity players needed to stay for their upcoming matches.

Jeff suggested they come to Ogden instead, only a 45 minute drive, and watch the remainder of their son's football game. Having overheard the conversation, Ardeth immediately asked Jeff to relay a message to Deb to bring

Kjrsten along to the football game as well. Jeff was having cell phone reception problems, so Ardeth called Deb directly.

The plans fell smoothly into place, and we were looking forward to sharing the second half of the seventh grade game together as a family. At halftime the CMB (Collins, Maxwell, and Baxter combined school districts for sports programs) Raiders held a less-than-commanding 8–0 lead.

***

Soon Hans' football game was over. The seventh grade Raiders won their first game of the season on the road against the Ogden Bulldogs 16–0. The players lined up after the game and proceeded in single file across the field to shake hands with their opponents. Returning to their side of the field for a post-game huddle, the celebration commenced. Twenty-six ecstatic seventh graders experiencing the 'thrill of victory' that would have made even Howard Cosell smile. Unfortunately, the CMB eighth graders were suffering the 'agony of defeat.'

But something was missing. Deb, Haley and Kjrsten still had not arrived and were now long overdue. Jeff called his wife on her cell phone but his coverage was not good and the calls wouldn't connect. Ardeth tried using her phone and finally got an answer on Deb's cell. "Deb?" Ardeth asked.

A man's voice responded, "Who is this?" "This is Ardeth." Silence. Then the man came back on the line. "Ma'am, I'm an EMT. There has been an accident, and we're treating the driver of the vehicle. The other passengers have been transported to the Boone County Hospital. That's all I can tell you."

For whatever reason, Ardeth didn't pursue additional information, simply acknowledging "Okay, we're on our way."

Hans and Mark were still celebrating in the back seat of the mini-van when we left for the Boone County Hospital. As we climbed in the van, I still remember Hans declaring, "This is the best day of my life" when he met me as he walked off the football field, following his team's first win of the season.

As we made our way to Boone, the adrenaline and enthusiasm gave way to caution, and the mood in the van quickly dampened. We had no idea what waited for us.

CHAPTER 5
LONG DAY'S JOURNEY INTO NIGHT...

I lift up my eyes to the mountains—where does my help come from? My help comes from the Lord, the Maker of heaven and earth.
Psalm 121:1, 2

September 16, 2004
Boone, Iowa

As the evening shadows lengthened, we called out to another parent, Sherry Samson before leaving the football field. Quickly, we asked her to notify the football coaches about the accident and to let them know that our son Hans and the Dillon's son, Mark, were riding with us. Because Jeff had ridden his motorcycle to the football game, his son Mark rode with us as we made our way to the hospital. We quickly piled into Grandma and Grandpa Hoeksema's mini-van and headed off for the Boone County Hospital with Hans and Mark still wearing their football uniform (pads, pants and cleats).

As the crow flies, Alleman (host town of the girls' volleyball game) is approximately 40 miles southeast of Ogden (host town of the boys' football game). However, driving the distance between the two towns requires using Highway 30 headed west, which skirts the southern edge of Boone. At this point, Highway 30 is four lanes with flashing lights and stop signs at a major intersection for access into town. Little did we know at the time, but that is the intersection where the accident occurred.

With what little information the EMT had provided us on the phone, we covered the 10 miles from Ogden to Boone driving east on Highway 30 towards Boone with only mild concern over the accident.

✳✳✳

Surely, they must have taken the girls to the hospital as a precaution for a cursory check-up following the accident. Ardeth called our pastor Jeff Sanderson to update him about the accident (even while we didn't yet have any details) and to please put Kjrsten on the prayer chain. As we approached the intersection on the edge of town, our hopes were soon crushed.

Distracted by the flashing lights of the emergency vehicles, I recall asking Ardeth, "Where's the car?" She pointed to the median and Deb's demolished green Ford Taurus. The emergency vehicles still at the scene of the crash and the condition of Deb's car left little doubt that someone could have suffered life-threatening injuries. The right rear end of the car was completely smashed—pushed deeply into the rear seat on the passenger side. The impact was so tremendous that Deb's Taurus had been thrown through the intersection, across the median and landing 90 degrees a kilter. I pulled over to the side of the highway, and the police officer directing traffic approached the driver's side of the mini-van warning me, "You can't stop there." Through eyes heavily clouded with tears, I quickly replied, "My daughter was in that car." He immediately ushered us through the intersection and directed us to the hospital.

(To view photographs of the vehicle, visit our website at www.MissionHillIowa.com)

Now we were truly alarmed, and our prayers intensified as we approached the hospital's emergency room just six blocks away.

It was nearly 7:30 pm when we arrived at the ER. The emergency room was hectic. We noticed a young man looking dazed and receiving treatment for minor scrapes while we were desperately trying to reunite with Kjrsten. We immediately identified ourselves to the hospital receptionist and requested to see our daughter.

"Which one is your daughter? Is she the blonde?" the nurse asked. "Our daughter is the 14-year-old," we replied anxiously. "We don't have any 14-year-olds. We're working on a 12-year-old." There was great confusion in the rush of the ER. Jeff arrived by motorcycle about the same time. We gave a detailed description of Kjrsten while at the same time Jeff was trying to describe his daughter Haley. Finally, after much heated discussion, Ardeth and I were allowed to enter the trauma room to see Kjrsten. Mark joined his dad and Hans stayed behind in the waiting room with Grandma and Grandpa Hoeksema.

It was a parent's worst nightmare. Three trauma nurses and one ER physician were working on Kjrsten. IV's had been inserted while the EKG monitor silently traced the beats of her heart. The doctor allowed us to come close while they continued the bag breathing and CPR compressions.

Side-by-side, my wife and I fell to our knees at the end of the gurney in that trauma room and begged God for a miracle. "Please don't take this child away from us. Please God. You are the Master Healer—heal her for us. Anything God, but please save our daughter."

***

As we prayed, the trauma team continued their life saving attempts. We were informed that the Life Flight helicopter had been sent from Des Moines and should be arriving in the next fifteen minutes. They needed to know which of the major hospitals in Des Moines was our choice for Kjrsten. Ardeth uttered a one-word answer, "Mercy." (Mercy Medical Center)

While Ardeth and I struggled inside the trauma room, Hans who had just turned 13 two weeks earlier was fighting his own battle outside in the waiting room. As observed by Grandma and Grandpa Hoeksema, Hans pleaded repeatedly, "God, please don't let my sister die." At one point, rocking back and forth on the floor with his elbows on his knees, he offered up the Lord's Prayer in earnest hope of God's mercy for Kjrsten—his only sister.

After what was in reality only a few minutes but felt like many more, Ardeth and I stood up. I moved closer to the head of the gurney where Kjrsten, with cascading blond hair lay motionless, while Ardeth stepped quietly to the side of the small trauma room. With her back to the wall, Ardeth then sank slowly to the floor—still hoping and praying for a miracle. One of the nurses saw Ardeth sitting there and thoughtfully handed her a damp cloth to wipe her tears. The early signs of emotional shock were already setting in as Ardeth later recalled the absolute numbness accompanied by uncertainty and then just the quiet.

Ardeth's mind wandered from one seemingly insignificant thought to another. 'Kjrsten, your nail polish on your toes needs to be re-done.' 'Why can I see that one big freckle on her knee since she's wearing jeans?' 'Oh-oh. They cut her favorite pair of jeans down the seams. This girl is going to be mad when she sees this.'

The thoughts just kept coming—no rhyme nor reason— just one distraught parent's mind trying desperately to make sense of it all and overcome the crushing fear.

***

As I continued to watch the trauma team working valiantly on Kjrsten, my eyes were riveted to the EKG monitor registering her heart blips. As I stared, the screen merged with the physician's CPR compressions, and I suddenly realized— the only time the screen blipped to register a heart beat was when the doctor compressed Kjrsten's chest. "Oh no," I murmured to no one but myself. I asked the physician the hardest question of my life, "Have there been any signs of life from this child since she was brought in?" It was not the answer we longed for. The emergency room doctor simply looked at me and quietly whispered, "No."

"Then let her go. She's already gone." The words were out of my mouth before I could catch them. The ER physician looked at the nurses and nodded, acknowledging my request. He silently moved away from Kjrsten and approached Ardeth and me. "Do you know anything about the accident?" he asked. We didn't. I walked over to Ardeth who sat stunned on the floor, still using the wall for support. "Ardeth, come here," I motioned and tried to help her off the floor.

The ER physician led us to the other side of the trauma room and pulled a curtain behind him creating a small private area. "The EMT team informed me that it took over twenty minutes from the time they arrived on the scene before they could cut your daughter free from the mangled backseat of the car. At that time she was not breathing. So, she had been without oxygen for at least that length of time. There is a very good chance she would have permanent brain damage if she could have been revived. And even without taking x-rays, it appears her neck is broken in two, maybe three places. Had she lived, she would have had severe paralysis." Then he said something I'll never forget, "I have a 14-year-old of my own too; I am so sorry," and he began to weep.

✳✳✳

Life Flight was just arriving when the order was given to send it back to Des Moines—empty. Little did Ardeth and I know at the time, but Hans along with Grandpa and Grandma Hoeksema had been sitting outside the emergency room in the parking lot when Life Flight arrived. The helicopter appeared on the scene and hovered briefly over the helipad for nearly a minute before suddenly departing. As Grandpa Marvin recounted later, "At that point we knew it was over."

Feeling numb, we left the makeshift office with the physician and returned to Kjrsten's side. Someone had now placed two chairs beside her gurney in the trauma room. We sat mostly in silence, broken by the nearly unceasing stream of tears and crying. I don't know for how long. It could have been 5 minutes or it might have been an hour. I finally reached out and touched Ardeth and reminded her that our son needed us. Ardeth rose from her chair and approached Kjrsten one last time, gently leaned down and kissed her forehead whispering her last words on earth to her daughter, "I'm going to miss you so much." Then we went to find Hans. In hindsight, we recognize what a miracle it was that my parents had been with us during the day and were able to be with Hans while we were in the trauma room that evening.

✳✳✳

It wasn't real. That was the over-riding sensation. It couldn't be happening. Not to us. We loved the Lord and had tried to faithfully serve Him all our adult lives—from teaching Sunday school to leading Bible study. Of course we knew we weren't perfect, but was this how God repays His own? The questioning began early and in earnest. The answers came much later—when they came at all.

We left the trauma room and found Hans in the parking lot with my parents. "Hans, Kjrsten didn't make it." There is no good way to tell a 13-year-old that his only sister had died in the horrific accident. Hans was distraught and naturally so. Growing up together and doing chores together, Kjrsten and Hans had forged a very close sibling relationship.

As his older sister, Kjrsten took great pains to be his protector or protagonist—depending on the situation. But God forbid that anyone else ever bother him. When Hans experienced challenges at school, she would encourage him by saying, "I know people—I have friends that will take care of things like this." Well, no friends could take care of this terminal situation now.

Hans insisted that he needed to see Kjrsten one last time. So he and I went back into the trauma room for a final goodbye. It wasn't long enough.

Hans looked at me and said, "But I don't want to be an only child." Ardeth stayed in the waiting room with my parents, and then called Pastor Jeff for a second time that evening. She had spoken with our pastor while en-route to the hospital before we knew the seriousness of the accident. "She didn't make it, Jeff," Ardeth told him. "What?!" Jeff exclaimed incredulously. The prayer chain at Bondurant Federated Church kicked into high gear. The prayers that didn't save Kjrsten were now going to be necessary to save what was left of our family. Jeff left Bondurant and headed to Boone to join us.

✳✳✳

A nurse approached Ardeth to start dealing with the paper work when Ardeth suddenly remembered that Kjrsten, just a few weeks earlier on August 3rd, had registered to be an organ donor at the time she received her driving permit. Immediately the pace quickened as the staff rushed to capture whatever could be saved from this tragedy. We were told someone would contact us later that evening from the Iowa Donor Network for answers to more questions.

As we waited to complete the release documents, the Iowa state trooper who had responded to the accident scene quietly approached us. He introduced himself and offered his condolences on our tragic loss. I asked him, "How did this happen?" He replied that the driver of the pickup truck claims he doesn't remember anything." "How can he not remember —he just killed my daughter!" The trooper patiently informed us that "an investigation is underway and when we get the completed accident report, I'll have more answers for you. We took blood tests from the driver, but the results won't be back for a few days. I will follow up with you as soon as I can. I am so sorry," he said and turned and walked away.

According to the trooper, Brian (last name withheld), then 28 years old, was driving a full-sized pick-up truck, traveling at 74 miles per hour when he slammed into the back of Deb's sedan while she and the girls were stopped at the intersection. There were no skid marks from the pickup truck and no attempt to stop. Kjrsten was sitting with Haley, in the rear passenger seat. Haley and her mother walked away— Kjrsten did not.

We had no answers—just lots of questions. How could this have happened?

✳✳✳

The reality of the evening was just beginning to set in, and it manifested itself physically. I couldn't breathe, my chest felt so tight. Every breath was a concentrated effort. How were we going to survive this? Did I even want to?

We had not seen any of the Dillon family since shortly after arriving in the hospital emergency room and being with Kjrsten and the trauma team. We were concerned about the Dillon's physical and emotional condition as well. Moving slowly down the ER hallway, we met Jeff and inquired about Haley and Deb. He informed us that Deb had suffered a significant cut on the back of her head that had needed staples as well as a cut on her foot. Haley had received some bumps and bruises.

Jeff asked about Kjrsten. "She didn't make it, Jeff," we told him. What could he say? Later we would come to understand that was a common reaction for all of us. We didn't know what to say either. We hardly felt anything except terrible numbness and deep exhaustion. The last thing I recalled was of Jeff offering his heartfelt condolences while asking us, "How am I going to tell them (his wife Deb and daughter Haley)?"

***

Our emotional systems were beginning to shut down as the shock settled in and the evening wore on. We knew it was time to leave. There was nothing left for us in Boone except a living nightmare.

Pastor Jeff was still driving towards Boone when we called him for a third time to let him know we were leaving the hospital. He immediately turned around and headed east to meet us at our home. Ardeth, Hans and I climbed into the minivan along with my parents and began the long journey back to Baxter.

Just as we were leaving the hospital, one of the nurses handed Ardeth Kjrsten's cell phone. It had been in her pocket, and the emergency response team had recovered it in the ER.

In the eerie quiet of the van in the dark of the night, the ring of Kjrsten's phone created a start. Ardeth answered and asked who was calling. It was Katie Van Zante—a friend, classmate and volleyball teammate. Katie was calling from the team bus, returning from the volleyball match that was nearing Baxter. Ardeth calmly informed Katie that she needed to talk to the coach. Katie relayed to Ardeth that "the coach was busy driving the bus." Ardeth firmly reiterated the need to talk to Coach Brook Byars, and Katie got her on the phone.

With amazing calmness and clarity Ardeth explained to Brook that, "Dillons (Deb and Haley) and Kjrsten were in an automobile crash, and Kjrsten did not survive." Then, her composure evaporated and her voice broke as she asked the coach, "How do I tell the girls?" Coach Byars assured Ardeth that she would handle it.

The following week, in her letter to Ardeth, Brook confided: "When I took your call last Thursday and you told me the terrible news, I was frightened and confused as to why I had to be the one with most of the girls that night. I wished I had been in a different place. But by the time I got the bus back to Baxter, I felt strength to tell the girls. I know now I was driving that bus for a reason."

✳✳✳

Only later did we learn that when the volleyball, football and the cross-country track team buses returned to Baxter, parents were already in town to meet them. The population of Baxter is around 1,100. Word spreads fast in a small town. With nearly every student carrying a cell phone, the word was out now and quickly spreading like wildfire.

The remainder of the ride home was a blur, only clearly illuminated by my parents' memories—and not revealed to us until months later. First we cried; then we prayed; and finally we sang. As unreal as that revelation sounds, even to us, Ardeth and I offered up songs of praise. As we drove home, we were not tuned into our favorite Christian radio station, KNWI 107.1—our singing was spontaneous. The Holy Spirit made a way, for even in the darkness of the night and our circumstances, to remember The Psalmist, "where does my help come from; my help comes from the Lord, maker of Heaven and earth." I think of Paul and Silas in jail and what did the Holy Spirit have them do? He directed them to pray and to sing. (Acts 16:25)

By the time we arrived home well after 10 pm that evening of September 16, our house was already filled with family and church friends. I recall listening to Ardeth's dad in our mudroom still shaking his head and saying, "I saw her this afternoon when I went up-town to the post office to get the mail. She was with a couple of her friends on the street by the school. I didn't even get to talk to her."

Ardeth's parents, Ard and Charlane Blomberg, had moved to Baxter earlier that same year after several years living in Macon, Georgia. Settling into retirement, they had purposely chosen Baxter as home base to be closer to their youngest grandchildren so they could spend more time with them. That long sought for reunion was short lived at best.

***

True to the nurse's word at the hospital in Boone, a representative from the Iowa Donor Network did call that evening with a host of questions. Thankfully, Kayla Erickson, a good friend from church and also a nurse, took the call and spent 20 minutes on the phone with the caller on our behalf.

Another act of kindness. Jesus said when you give even a cup of water in my name, you will be rewarded. Through Kjrsten's decision to be an organ donor, many others received medical gifts.

To this day, so much of that fateful evening is still a hazy memory. It was well after midnight before everyone left our home. When Ardeth and I finally laid down to rest, we felt defeated—spiritually, emotionally and physically. We had nothing left.

But even in the midst of one the worst possible experiences a parent can endure, God was still with us. In 2003, Ardeth and I were leaders of a couple's small group study on "Divorce Proof Your Marriage." It was a study guide prepared by Dr. Gary and Barb Rosberg with America's Family Coaches. What God brought to us that night was a chapter from that study that dealt with the storms of life. In the study guide Gary wrote, "If you're not in a storm, or have never been through a storm, get ready; because one is coming. It's not a question of if, but only when. And when that storm hits, you can allow that storm to drive a wedge between you and your spouse or you can let it slam you together and meld an even stronger relationship."

Little did we know at the time but later learned, 80 percent of marriages that suffer the loss of a child end in divorce. We looked at each other that night and vowed that we would not allow this to destroy our marriage. We would not allow this nightmare to destroy our family. And, we would not allow this tragedy to separate us from our faith. It was a short prayer but covered all the important issues.

The chorus of a song recorded by Christian artist Matt Redman, 'Blessed Be Your Name' exemplifies our state of mind during those dark days: *Blessed be your name. He gives and takes away. He gives and takes away. My heart will choose to say; blessed be your name, Jesus.*

Later that same night, my mother had a vision. She watched in awe as a bright and illuminating light shone atop a high mountain, and the skies opened, and Heaven welcomed Kjrsten. It wasn't until seven years later that my mother shared that vision with me.

CHAPTER 6

LETTING GO

The Lord gave and the Lord has taken away;
may the name of the Lord be praised.
Job 1:21b

Friday, September 17
Baxter Iowa

The only sleep came in the form of utter exhaustion. There was no rest. How do you start a new life? I couldn't fathom where to begin. I had known beyond a shadow of a doubt that we had been truly and graciously blessed for years. And we thanked God every day for His blessings. We had the perfect family. I had a wonderful wife; two terrific children; a successful business. What more could a man ask? I recall sharing with my friends that I had everything a man could want. My job was done. I could die a happy man knowing that my children knew Jesus personally as their Lord and Savior.

But while I may have been content dying, I wasn't content with my daughter dying.

On Friday morning we found ourselves going through the motions. No clear idea of exactly what to do but recognizing that making funeral arrangements was our first priority. My parents came to the house and stayed with Hans as we had made an appointment for early that afternoon with the funeral director. But Ardeth believed there were higher priorities. First we drove to the school to check on Kjrsten's closest friends. We talked briefly with Superintendent Neil Seals who informed us that the local television media had been inquiring about visiting the school as well as interviewing us. As far as we were concerned, "If it was fine with the school, it was fine with us."

✳✳✳

Ardeth felt very strongly that we also needed to connect with Deb Dillon, the driver of the car in which Kjrsten had been killed by a reckless driver the prior evening.

"I want to make sure Deb knows this was not her fault and that we do not feel any ill will toward her. I just need to tell her," Ardeth explained. So we drove to the home of Jeff and Deb Dillon on the outskirts of Baxter the morning after the accident to offer what little comfort we could to their family. The events of the previous evening had upset their lives as well as ours. Coincidentally, September 16th is their daughter Haley's birthday. While Haley survived the crash with bumps and bruises, the emotional damage of reliving the event every birthday thereafter would likely be far greater than could be imagined.

As we approached their home and rang the doorbell, Jeff answered the front door. Deb hung way back in the foyer, not sure how this visit would play out. Ardeth immediately went to Deb, and with a hug and eyes full of tears assured her that we were not angry with them and would be praying for them as they struggled through this tragedy as well. We didn't stay long. We shared what the Iowa state trooper had told us, briefly compared notes with what he had related to them and headed back home to begin work on the funeral arrangements.

With so many unwelcome tasks looming, looking back at the visit that morning with the Dillon family, it seemed so out of sync. At the time it just seemed to be the right thing to do. Both families desperately needed to begin the painful process of healing and recovery from this unexpected nightmare.

As we drove home, Ardeth and I talked about Brian, the reckless young man who had killed our daughter. The same young man in the hospital emergency room receiving treatment while we struggled with the nurse for admittance to see our daughter in the same emergency room the night before. The young man who (we learned later) was high on meth,prescription meds and driving with no insurance when he took our daughter's life. And we prayed in the car, "God, please do not let us hate. And please, God, do not let this make us bitter people. We do not want to live our lives that way."

Amazingly, God answered that prayer almost from the beginning. Neither of us was able to bring ourselves to hate Brian. He had wronged us terribly and forever changed our lives for the worse. But if our faith meant anything, we had to forgive. If we desired God's forgiveness, we had to extend forgiveness. In the emergency room the night before, we had pleaded with God for a miracle healing of our daughter. In God's sovereignty we did not receive that miracle. But we did receive His miracle this morning—we were able to let go of the natural feelings of anger, disgust and hatred towards

Brian. And even now I thank God daily for making that possible because left to my own desires, it would have been too easy to hate.

***

Who could know how much work was involved in making funeral arrangements for a vibrant young woman who had been healthy and full of life just the day before? We hadn't reserved cemetery plots because those were for aged people. Our grieving time was devoted to finding a funeral home, choosing a casket, writing a eulogy, selecting photos for a PowerPoint and a host of other exhausting tasks. In the midst of this frenzy, our home was also a beehive of comers and goers. All shared the same sentiment, 'how could this be happening?'

Pastor Jeff Sanderson was a great blessing during the early hours of this unexpected journey. So much of it simply felt like we were going through the motions. And the myriad of necessary decisions felt insurmountable at times.

Something as straight forward as choosing a casket. It was so difficult. So many choices. How do you decide? And so incredibly expensive. Because Kjrsten was only five feet tall, we bought a youth casket in periwinkle blue—her favorite color.

We knew it would be a closed casket service, not because as many speculated that she had been badly bruised and disfigured in the crash but because we wanted her friends to remember her smiling and alive. The way we knew she was in Heaven just at the moment. It was important to us that for those of us left behind, our last visual memory of Kjrsten be connected to 'life' and not death.

Friday night football is a sacred event for most small towns in the Midwest, and Baxter was no exception. It was part date night, part social gathering and part about bragging rights for the coming week. This Friday night was about to be shaken. For one of the rare times in Iowa sports history, a football game was postponed. Here was the challenge: CMB Raiders were to play an away game against the Bondurant Blue Jays. Kjrsten went to school at Baxter, the 'B' of CMB. but she went to church, Sunday school and youth group in Bondurant. Both student bodies were suffering greatly from yesterday's loss. Consequently, the game was postponed until the following Monday evening, the day scheduled for Kjrsten's funeral.

Because of the nature of the accident and that it involved a child fatality, the story had hit the local television news media. Television crews arrived in Baxter to interview anyone willing to speak about the accident. Reporters for WOI–TV channel 5 called the house to arrange an interview with Ardeth and me. We consented and answered their questions as best we could despite our still numb state of emotions.

(To view local television coverage, visit our website at www.MissionHillIowa.com)

***

Saturday was packed with visitors. I reflect on all the acts of kindness displayed those first couple of days. Mary Madsen came to the house, made lunch for us, and left. It was the first meal we had eaten since Thursday noon. Kayla Erickson delivered Kjrsten's clothes to the funeral home for us. Ardeth's brother Curtis drove down from Minneapolis to the local florist's shop and spent an entire day arranging flowers for the funeral. There were too many to mention them all. And I fear I may not have thanked them at the time, but we deeply appreciated their support.

In some ways, part of me felt sorry for our guests as they struggled to find something to say to ease our suffering. And well-meaning folks managed to say some of the worst things possible.

"You have an angel now in Heaven looking out for you." Not known for quietly keeping my opinions to myself, I felt obligated to point out that angels were created beings as were humans but entirely separate. Or, "You have a God who knows what it's like to lose a child" to which I retorted, "Give me my daughter back in three days, and we'll call it good." Or, the one that topped it all off, "Having this beautiful house in this park-like setting will surely be a comfort to you in this time of struggle." How do you respond to that?

I found the greatest support came from those who said very little except to say, "I have no idea what you're going through—my heart just breaks for you." And they would cry with us. I especially remember my brother John who simply sat on the fireplace hearth most of the day not saying anything. Just being there was John's way of supporting us.

✳✳✳

Another ray of encouragement God provided came from our son Hans. Throughout the day on Saturday, many of Hans' classmates came with their parents to show their concern. At one point I remember looking out the window and seeing Hans and Marcus Schmidt playing catch with a football. Even laughing together. And then I realized, someday we too will still experience joy. I didn't know when, but I knew it was out there and still very much a part of God's plan for our lives. God's blessing was still upon us, and we made it a conscious point to continually remind ourselves of that fact.

I wandered out of the house to get away from all the commotion. My oldest brother Steve followed as we meandered aimlessly, finally standing just outside the barn. I reminded Steve of something he had shared with me 22 years earlier. Steve and his wife Cindy lost their first child, Aaron, to spina bifida shortly after his birth. I was attending William Penn University in Oskaloosa when I heard the news. I immediately headed for the hospital where Steve met me coming through the visitor entrance doors. He looked me in the eye, and before I could say a word, he admonished me "Dave, don't be mad at God." I couldn't believe what I was hearing. My brother had just lost his first child at birth, but his faith was unshaken.

Now here I was in the same situation. We talked some more, and I shared a thought that had been germinating since the accident. In all of the inner turmoil raging in my spirit, one burning thought kept surfacing. "I believe I will come to know the Lord in a way I could never have before this tragedy." I wasn't sure how or what that would look like, but I believed that if I allowed Him to, God was preparing to reveal some kingdom secrets.

Late that morning, Jeff Dillon dropped off Kjrsten's

belongings, having driven back to Boone to retrieve them from the wrecked car. Her gym bag was filled with volleyball gear and her backpack with school paraphernalia. The old adage came to my mind—if you want to know someone's priorities, don't search any further than their checkbook. In Kjrsten's case, all that was necessary was a quick glance at her daily planner. As Ardeth and I flipped through the pages of the planner, we were struck with the notations. Clever little sayings penciled in the margins; dates of upcoming tests or important assignments; and 6:30 pm every Sunday night reserved for 'youth group.' That was one of her priorities.

***

Kjrsten loved the Lord Jesus Christ. And she had a tremendous burden for her friends' salvation. On more than one occasion she confessed to Ardeth that she was worried that many of her friends did not know the Lord as their personal savior. Where would they spend eternity? Dale Johnson, her Sunday school teacher, recounted to us years later that Kjrsten sometimes felt as though she was the only Christian in her school (besides her brother she admitted). As parents and followers of Christ, Ardeth and I encouraged Kjrsten to live her life as an example Christ would be proud of and to pray faithfully for her friends.

Some of the contents of Kjrsten's gym bag were more difficult to handle than others. For Kjrsten's thirteenth birthday, her mother and I took her shopping for a promise ring. We encouraged her to choose something that she would be proud to wear on the ring finger of her left hand as a sign

56

that she was choosing to remain pure, saving herself only for her husband. Later it would be replaced with an engagement ring and then the wedding band. Kjrsten chose a small blue sapphire with two diamonds surrounding it on either side. It was a beautiful symbol of her commitment that her friends admired and it seldom left her finger.

Now we couldn't find it anywhere. Ardeth checked on the registry of Kjrsten's personal effects with the hospital in Boone. The ring had not been on her finger. The ring was missing. But as God's grace would have it, one of her friends, Jenn Saak was at the house helping Ardeth go through Kjrsten's gym bag. Amazingly, Jenn found it tucked safely away.

Discovering that Kjrsten's voice mail message was still intact on her cellular phone was a huge find. You wouldn't think a cell phone was such a big deal but for us it proved monumental. It permanently recorded her voice! When a parent loses a child, one of the greatest fears is that the person who was loved so much would be forgotten. For us, having preserved her voice message was like discovering a gold mine. Her brother Hans managed to transfer Kjrsten's voice message to his cell phone. For several years callers to Hans' phone would be surprised with a female voice answering, "Hi, this is Kit's phone. Leave a message and I'll call you back." (Kit was her nickname to all her friends.) Thanks to technology, Kjrsten "Kit" Hoeksema was gone but not forgotten.

✳✳✳

Ardeth and I were the Sunday school teachers for the fifth and sixth grade children in our church. But on this painful

Sunday morning, we couldn't bring ourselves to teach. Close friends Jared and Kayla Erickson graciously filled in for us. However, we did manage to drag ourselves to church. It is very difficult to bring yourself to a place of praise when in your heart all you feel is hurt, betrayal and anger. We learned firsthand not to trust feelings at a time like this but to trust in the promises of God.

Rich Mullins expressed it so well in his song: 'My Deliverer' *He will never break His promise. Though I doubt my heart; I doubt my eyes.*

Even when what I see and feel all around me causes me to doubt, the one thing I must trust is His promises.

Thankfully, we serve a patient God who loves us even in our worst times. I thank God that He never gave up on us even when we may have fleetingly wanted to give up on Him. That morning, maybe more than at any other time in our lives, we needed to be reassured that God was God; and that He was still on His throne; and still very much in charge.

And we needed to worship. We needed the love and caring concern of our extended church family. And they needed to see us too. We weren't the only ones in great pain that first Sunday. So many young people (and old as well) were desperately trying to grasp how this senseless tragedy could be allowed to happen.

Pastor Jeff came out to the house on Sunday afternoon to review final arrangements for the visitation and the funeral which was scheduled for Monday. We handed off a hundred or so photographs that Jeff Vargason graciously put into a power point set to the music of Steven Curtis Chapman's 'Fingerprints of God.' To this day, my brother John finds it impossible to listen to that song. Half jokingly, he told me years later, "Thanks for ruining that song for me forever." Kjrsten used to love good-natured teasing with Uncle John. They were close, and it hit him very hard.

(To view the power point presentation, visit our website at www.MissionHillIowa.com)

As Pastor Jeff, Ardeth and I talked about the order of service for the funeral planned for Monday, I shared with Jeff that I wanted to speak to the attendees at the service. Pastor Jeff thought that was probably not a wise idea. But I have rarely been as convicted about something as I was about this. I was emphatic, "We are not going to lose an opportunity to share the gospel of Jesus Christ with all those youth who will be in attendance." Jeff finally conceded, with the caveat that if the time came and I didn't feel I could carry through, just give him a nod, and he'd move on.

✳✳✳

The visitation on Sunday was scheduled for family between 4 and 5 pm. Several asked why we chose to have a closed casket. Was it because she was so badly beaten up in the accident? The simple answer was 'No.' Kjrsten's physical appearance after the accident had not changed. Her injuries were internal and not visible. Our decision was based solely on our desire that her friends remember her as the vivacious young woman she was, not the shell that had been left behind. The memory we all needed to take with us was Kjrsten celebrating life—real life with Jesus Christ. So we placed a large framed photograph on the casket—one with Kjrsten's unforgettable smile.

Visitation for guests was slated between the hours of 5 to 7 pm. In actuality, guests began arriving at 4:30 that afternoon; and when the last of the visitors left, it was nearly 9 pm. We had no idea how long the line was until later. Friends shared with us how they had waited for nearly three hours in the receiving line in the church—a line that extended around the block and the adjacent parking lot. While Ardeth and I were inside the sanctuary, Hans busied himself by roaming the line, greeting and hugging family and friends and occasionally muttering to no one in particular, "I hate this; I hate this."

The outpouring of support was amazing. More than 80 live floral arrangements from friends, family, clients, volleyball teams from surrounding schools and others graced the front of the church. At the visitation, Father Kiernan, a priest I had closely worked with at Holy Family Catholic School in Des Moines, offered me an interesting analogy, "You have just gone through crucifixion; Kjrsten has just gone through the resurrection." He was correct; Kjrsten had won, but that left us as the big losers.

✱✱✱

One of the most moving moments of the evening was the result of Kjrsten's closest friends and other members of her volleyball team, presenting Ardeth, Hans and me with a large poster photograph of Kjrsten in uniform serving the volleyball, with a caption that read 'Now playing on God's team.' Many of the girls, after waiting in line for several hours, simply sat in the front row pews of the sanctuary and supported us as we continued to greet visitors.

After the Sunday visitation that lasted far into the evening, as Ardeth, Hans, and I drove home, we talked about the experience. We all had the same feeling. It was true. God had allowed us to reach out and give comfort to so many that night with the reassurance that God was still in control, and we were His children. In the big picture, nothing had changed. Go figure.

Weeks, months and even years later, people would comment to Ardeth and me about how strong you were that night. I always responded with the words from a Twila Paris song, *Deep inside this armor, the warrior is a child*. If we exhibited any strength that night, it wasn't ours. All credit goes to the Holy Spirit and to Him be the glory.

As the weekend drew to a close, our family—now reduced to three—knew that Monday would be our most difficult day without Kjrsten—a day of truly letting go.

CHAPTER 7

HEAVEN'S GATE

"Truly I tell you, today you will be with me in paradise."
Luke 23:43

Monday, September 20, 2004
Bondurant Federated Church

Now there were just three. The house seemed so empty. It was impossible to fathom the loss and change that was now being forced upon, in my mind, our 'once perfect family of four.' The reality of the changes in our lives were only now beginning to surface. I would never have the opportunity to walk my daughter down the aisle. We had lost half of our opportunity for future grandchildren. All the responsibility for looking after mom and dad as they grew older would now fall onto Hans.

In my mind I repeatedly replayed the same sentiments: I miss you; I miss what could have been; I miss what would have been; I miss what should have been.

Most difficult of all was the realization that no matter what happened from this day forward, it would never be as good as it had been just four days earlier. I knew there would be joy. I knew there were blessings God still had in store for us. But no matter how good that would be, it would never compare to when we were whole as a family. I knew we were damaged goods. We were the amputee who would learn to live without his legs but knew he'd never run a marathon as he had before. I think those were the most depressing thoughts and feelings—the sense that the best days of your life have suddenly and without warning come to an end, and you are facing the downward side of life. I expect everyone reaches that place in life, due to advancing age or health concerns. I just never expected to be hit so hard by it so soon.

***

My father Marvin and I were standing on the back porch of the house, just off the kitchen. As we looked to the north and into our timbered pasture, we watched the cattle grazing peacefully on the hillside. But there was no peace in my heart. I was angry. And I wanted God to know it. When I finally stopped railing on about the unfairness of God, my father asked a very simple and pointed question. "So what are you going to do—abandon your faith?"

Initially, I was insulted by the question but it forced me to consider my options. There really was nothing to consider. I immediately confirmed, more for me than for him, that I could not abandon my faith. It would be easier to stop breathing than to stop believing.

But this scenario played out again and again over the years. From that time on, Ardeth and I were cautious about sharing our deepest feelings of anger, betrayal, confusion and hurt toward God with others for fear they would jump to the conclusion that we were in fact abandoning our faith. We were committed for the long haul to Jesus Christ, but that didn't stop the questions from creeping into our lives.

***

The funeral service for Kjrsten was scheduled for 10:00 am at Bondurant Federated Church. Our family had been active in the church since moving to Iowa from Minnesota in 2000. The church building had recently been expanded with a new sanctuary. Now it held over 600 friends, family and fellow students. Today, folding seats had been set up in the narthex to accommodate the crowd.

Ironically, our church is located directly across the street from what was then the Bondurant High School. The high school Assistant Principal, Mike Kramer is a friend and member of our church. Most of our church youth group was comprised of kids from the Bondurant School. But today the church was packed with kids from two student bodies, representing Kjrsten's church family of friends from Bondurant and her school family of friends from Collins, Maxwell and Baxter (CMB).

We knew how much Kjrsten's loss meant to us, but we were only just beginning to understand the full impact of her life and subsequent loss on her classmates.

As with the visitation, we decided on a closed casket at the final farewell so that the lasting image of Kjrsten was to be of her alive and vibrant.

Shortly before entering the sanctuary and beginning our

long slow walk to the front of the church, we had one last time of prayer with Pastor Jeff. Once again Jeff asked if I was determined to address the gathered mourners personally. I assured Jeff I had never felt so strongly about anything in my life. Jeff gave me one last out, "Just before we ask you to speak, I'll look at you and if you change your mind, just give me a nod, and I'll move on." That wasn't going to happen.

***

There is no such thing as a good funeral. But I believe some are better than others. And I have come to understand the underlying difference is 'Hope.' We were the fortunate ones. We knew beyond a shadow of a doubt where Kjrsten was that day—waiting for us at Heaven's Gate. That promise of hope is also what made it easier for Pastor Jeff to talk about Kjrsten because he knew her and knew her well.

He highlighted tidbits from Kjrsten's daily planner. She had 'Youth Group' written in every Sunday night and 'Church' penciled in every Sunday morning. Or the amazing story of what she scribbled in her planner on the day her life was cut short. Kjrsten had written the chorus lyrics to the song 'Love, Me' by Collin Raye: *If you get there before I do. Don't give up on me. I'll meet you when my chores are through; I don't know how long I'll be. But I'm not going to let you down; darling wait and see. Cause between now and then, 'til I see you again; I'll be loving you — love me.*

Kjrsten loved living in the country, and she loved country music too.

Ardeth often reflects back on those chorus words written

by Kjrsten on the day she left, as her goodbye note to us only written in reverse.

If I get there before you do. Don't give up on you. I'll meet you when your chores are through; I don't know how long you'll be. But you're not going to let me down; dad-mom-Hans wait and see. Cause between now and then, 'til I see you again; I'll be loving you— love, me.

✳✳✳

Pastor Jeff was passionate at the memorial service. He acknowledged the superintendent from Baxter to commend him in public, for in Jeff's words, "Showing that a life is worth more than a game" with the school administration's decision to postpone the scheduled football game. He understood and shared about Kjrsten's commitment to Christ. Jeff shared the story about when Kjrsten was the first one in line to sign up for the youth group's mission trip. She couldn't wait to be included in the following summer's trip a trip she'd now— never be able to take.

And then it was time. Pastor Jeff looked at me, and I stood up from the front row and slowly climbed the five steps to the sanctuary stage. I had contemplated putting my thoughts into a written outline but was worried I may not be able to read my notes through the tears. In the end, I opted to simply leave it in the hands of the Holy Spirit.

I began by speaking directly to the students. "I'm sure you all expected to hear from a pastor today about things of heaven and God, but I want you to hear from a grieving father. And to hear something I believe is really important. The first thing

I want to say is this does not change who God is. He is the same today as He was last Thursday.

God loves me, Ardeth and Hans as much today as He did when Kjrsten was still with us. And He loves each of you just as much. We serve an awesome God. And speaking for Ardeth and Hans, we recognize we have been incredibly blessed. This tragedy does not change that.

God is still on His throne and He is still sovereign.

Those of you who knew Kjrsten have commented over and over to us how she was so full of life. She was bubbly, spontaneous and her joy was contagious. You're smiling right now because you know it's true. But did you ever stop and ask where that joy came from?

Jesus said 'I came to give life and give it abundantly.' That's where the joy in her life came from!

This is the absolute worst time in my life right now. But one of the things that makes it bearable is knowing that Kjrsten knew Jesus Christ as her Lord and Savior. Right now, that is the greatest comfort we can find at a time like this.

I want to challenge you young people here today. You don't know what tomorrow holds. We all think we do. We make plans and fill our calendars well into the future. But the truth is, you don't know if you're getting home today. When Kjrsten left the volleyball game, she was sure she was going to arrive safely home that night. Unfortunately, she didn't make it home—at least not to her earthly home. She did however make it to her heavenly home because of a conscious decision she made years ago to accept Jesus Christ as her Lord and Savior. And if you don't know where you will spend eternity if something happens to you today, as it did to Kjrsten last Thursday, don't you leave here until you do."

Then it was time to speak directly to the parents. "Do you know where your kids are at with their faith? Do you talk to them? I would occasionally ask Hans and Kjrsten as we were driving down the road "Do you know the Lord?" An in unison reply of "You know we do" would echo from the back seat. It reached the point where they tired of my asking. But I never tired of their response.

We are positive that Kjrsten had invited Jesus to be Lord of her life because we were there when she made that decision. Little did we know then how important those little conversations would be in the near future. Talk to your kids. Ask them regularly. Because you do not want to someday be standing in our shoes and wondering 'Did my child know the Lord?'"

I finally closed with verses 6 & 7 from John chapter 14, "I am the way and the truth and the life. No one comes to the father except through me. If you really knew me, you would know my Father as well.' Those of you who knew Kjrsten and that spirit of joy got a glimpse of her heavenly Father."

***

Over the years I have had countless number of people ask me, "How could you get up and speak at your own daughter's funeral?" The truthful answer is, "How couldn't I get up and speak?" I have been asked to fill the pulpit on occasion when our pastor has been away. At those times I worry and labor for weeks on preparing and then delivering those sermons. But this day was different. Never had I been more convicted that this is what God wanted me to do and that He would supply the words. It was in that way, one of the easiest messages I have ever delivered.

(For an audio of David's comments or the entire service, visit our website at www.MissionHillIowa.com)

Pastor Jeff closed the service with a special invitation. He had prepared little yellow postcards that were distributed in every pew in the sanctuary. "The cards," Jeff explained to the audience, "offer the opportunity to do several things. First, I'm going to pray for anyone wishing to receive Jesus this morning as Savior and Lord. If you want the promise and assurance of eternal life that David was talking about, pray with me now. Please indicate that decision on the card. There is also a space where you can write a note to David, Ardeth and Hans if you'd like. We're going to collect these shortly and will give them to the Hoeksemas to keep."

Later that week when we finally sat down and took the time to read each one of those cards, there were 234 checkmarks on the line 'Today, I want you to know that I invited Jesus Christ to be my Savior and Lord!' Another miracle. What Satan had meant for evil, God had intended for His glory.

There were many notes included on those cards that touched our hearts. "Thank you for showing me that death doesn't have to be depressing." "Thank you for showing me the way to Jesus today."

At the suggestion of my brother John, we chose Mercy Me's 'I Can Only Imagine' and Kjrsten's former school choir director sang it solo. John thought it was a good fit.

At the conclusion of the funeral service, Ardeth, Hans and

I climbed in the funeral limo and rode the 21 miles from Bondurant to the Baxter cemetery. Again I was struck by what a beautiful late summer day it was. Sunny and warm. I kept thinking it should be grey and cold to match my spirit.

Again, it was little acts of kindness on that day that stood out in my memory. Our neighbor in the country, Mike Brandt, said he'd be honored if he could help with the funeral procession. He, along with our Baxter City police officer Steve Wright, led the convoy that was two miles long and helped cordon off key intersections along the route.

✳✳✳

As we gathered at the gravesite, my beloved wife was overcome with emotion. As she watched the pallbearers, consisting of our respective brothers and our eldest nephew, carry the coffin of our daughter to the resting place under the tent, the gravity of her new life buckled her knees and she collapsed to the ground. I quickly rushed to support her and she raised both hands toward Heaven and implored, "God, please help us through this." As she shared with me later, she was faced with the finality of it all—besides suffering the loss of her only daughter, she had also lost her best friend.

The volleyball team and Kjrsten's closest friends silently filed past the coffin, each one gently placing a rose on the top of the closed casket. Good days were still to come, but without a doubt, the best days were past.

There was no head stone as we hadn't had time to select one yet. But I remember feeling there should be something there. The fear of Kjrsten being forgotten was already beginning to creep into my mind. Oh, there were lots of notes and flowers left behind, but for us it would never be enough.

Following the brief gravesite service, we headed back to Bondurant for a luncheon reception at the church. By this time, we were quite exhausted and the potluck meal was a blur. We still didn't have much appetite and spent most of our time feeling as though we were the ones making the effort to console those around us who struggled to comfort us. What a strange, but I understand common, reflex.

The luncheon did provide an opportunity to finally look into the faces of those friends in attendance. The funeral was so large and our time and attention were so compartmentalized, I wasn't sure who actually attended the service. For weeks afterwards, I would run into friends and clients who would comment to me about the funeral, and I wasn't even aware they had been there.

For several hours we circulated around the fellowship hall and visited. Many of our dear friends from Minnesota made the effort to come, and that meant a great deal to us. But we were quickly wearing out with need to retreat back to our home that has always been our safe haven. This time it felt awkward with an extra chair at the kitchen table that would forevermore be empty.

Late in the afternoon, the deacons asked if they could come out and pray with us. We naturally agreed but made it clear, the visit would have to be brief as we had plans later that evening. It was, after all, the rescheduled football game between Bondurant and CMB. And we had been told there were plans to honor Kjrsten at the beginning of the game.

***

As we arrived at the Bondurant football field, the local media was already there filming background and getting interviews. The story of Kjrsten's death had been on the news most of the weekend, and now the focus of the story was of the rare occasion that a game was postponed–making state sports history. We made our way to the visitor stands while quietly acknowledging the nodded greetings and murmured hellos. Shortly before kick off, the announcer called for a moment of silence in Kjrsten's honor. Everyone stood, caps came off, and heads bowed. It was another quiet goodbye.

One of the reporters for WHO-TV channel 13, Mark Tauschek asked in one of his interviews how the family was holding up. The interviewee told him that they were there in the stands, and he could ask them himself. Mark came over and introduced himself, and we consented to an interview. "Some would ask what are you doing here tonight when you just buried your daughter this morning?" asked Mark. "This is where Kjrsten would have been," we answered.

We discovered that Mark is an extremely compassionate and caring individual who for months afterwards would on occasion call Ardeth just to check up on us. Another (not random) act of kindness.

For the life of me, I couldn't remember who won the game that night. But Ardeth remembered clearly that CMB won. In fact, they scored five touchdowns. She likes to think it was one for each year Kjrsten started school in Baxter (5th, 6th, 7th, 8th, and 9th grades).

That fall CMB sports season witnessed numerous tributes

to Kjrsten and her life at Baxter. Her volleyball team ordered special T-shirts with her number and nickname (Kit) printed on the sleeves. Collette Kunkel, one of the volleyball team mothers, had special pins created with black and silver ribbons and Kjrsten's #11 inside.

Even the cross country squad adopted black bands with Kjrsten's initials. And the junior high football team had #11 for Kjrsten printed on their helmets as well. All except for Hans, who simply said, "I don't need a number on my helmet to remember my sister."

← Newlyweds—
Mr. and Mrs.
David Hoeksema.

Just the
two of us

↑ Enjoying some fun in the sun.

↑ Traveling together.

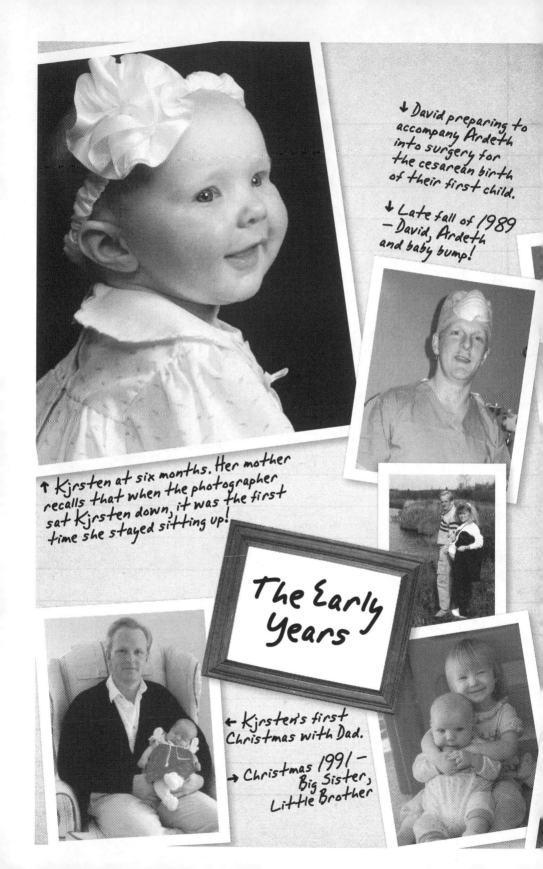

↓ David preparing to accompany Ardeth into surgery for the cesarean birth of their first child.

↓ Late fall of 1989 — David, Ardeth and baby bump!

↑ Kjrsten at six months. Her mother recalls that when the photographer sat Kjrsten down, it was the first time she stayed sitting up!

The Early Years

← Kjrsten's first Christmas with Dad.

→ Christmas 1991 — Big Sister, Little Brother

→ In preparation for a friend's wedding, Ardeth and friend Tami created a white suit for Hans and paired it with a ruffled lace and satin dress for Kjrsten.

↑ The Hoeksema's family of four — David, Ardeth, Hans and Kjrsten

↑ David and Hans cooking together.

← Kjrsten's first day of kindergarten. Pre-screening revealed "lazy eye" requiring treatment with patching.

↑ As a road warrior, David logged more than a million Frequent Flyer miles, making it possible for the entire family to travel for educational and recreational purposes — always with the idea of creating relationships and making memories.

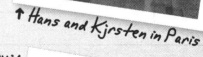

← David and Kjrsten dancing on first cruise.

↑ Hans and Kjrsten in Paris

→ Kjrsten, David and Hans hanging out on Labadee, a port on the northern coast of Haiti.

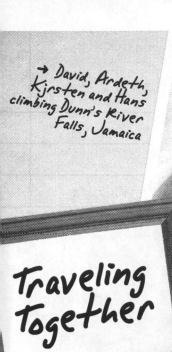

→ David, Ardeth, Kjrsten and Hans climbing Dunn's River Falls, Jamaica

Traveling Together

↑ Kjrsten and David — Friends, May 2004

↑ Kjrsten and Hans enrolled in a Beluga Whale Encounter, San Antonio, Texas

↓ Kjrsten loved Ardeth's Mustang.

↑ Kjrsten enjoying a malt in Kansas City — proudly wearing her "promise ring."

Growing Older

↓ David and Kjrsten cooking together

← Father and daughter all dressed up for 'Daddy Date-Night — an annual tradition for celebrating Kjrsten's birthday.

→ Kjrsten and Ardeth
— best friends!

↑ First day of school
for Kjrsten and Hans

↑ Kjrsten posed for the
volleyball team photos while
sporting a shoulder tattoo
as an artful tribute to the
Iowa State Cyclones.

↓ Even a hobby farm is always a work in progress!

↓ I am laughing, dancing and singing praises to my Lord and Savior! I look forward to the day we are reunited in heaven. "If you confess with your mouth and believe in your heart that Jesus is Lord you will be saved." Romans 10:9

(from the back of Kjrsten's headstone)

If you get there before I do don't ~~let~~ give up on me. I'll meet you when my chores are thru. I don't kno how long I'll be but I'm not gonna let you down wait for...♪♪

16 THURSDAY

Aig. 11 - choir. review 2:49

17 FRIDAY

↑ Kjrsten's freshman Daily Planner from September 16th inspired this book.

↑ Kit's Courtyard

Living with No Regrets

↓ Family of three — 2009

↓ David and Ardeth

CHAPTER 8

THE GOD OF ALL COMFORT

For the Lord is good and his love endures forever;
his faithfulness continues through all generations.
Psalm 100:5

Tuesday, September 21st–Sunday, October 3rd
Baxter, Iowa

Now came the hard part—how to start living again when the last thing I wanted to do was to go on living. The funeral was over; the visitors were gone. Very quickly it became quiet and lonely.

The loneliness and depression at times were unbearable, creating frequent unhealthy thoughts. For months after Kjrsten's death when I found myself meeting a semi-trailer truck on the highway, I would tell myself how easy it would be to simply tweak the steering wheel to the left and the pain would be over in an instant. However, suicide would only compound the hurt in those I loved most and thankfully God did not allow those thoughts to take root.

Hans had school; I had work. But for too much of the time Ardeth had a quiet, empty house filled only with memories.

I was often asked how I kept the business afloat after

Kjrsten died. As a sole proprietor who worked out of his home office, I was the business. If I didn't show up and perform, there was no fall back or contingency plan. So consequently I returned to work on Wednesday—two days after Kjrsten's funeral. It would have been easy and certainly tempting to say 'I quit.' But I actually believe it was helpful for me—it was the daily distraction and routine I needed to create some sense of order in the midst of the grieving storm.

✳✳✳

Hans returned to school the same day I returned to work. He insisted on going back to classes. Sitting at home and watching his parents grieve and not knowing what to do with so much time on his hands was taking its toll. Those first days back at school were excruciatingly difficult for Hans. He came home after the second day and broke down, "I caught myself all day looking for Kjrsten in the hallway. I never knew how much we saw each other passing between classes until now when I can't see her in the halls. I don't want to go back."

But go back he did the very next day. Ardeth called the school to give them a 'heads-up' that Hans really didn't want to be there. Lisa Cross, the school guidance counselor, pulled Hans out of class and took time to just sit and talk to him. She shared with Ardeth later the same haunting words Hans had told us the night before, "where Kjrsten should have been, she wasn't."

Hans' football coach understood some of what Hans was experiencing, having lost a sister himself. As the rest of the team members rode the bus to the practice field after school,

Bob Cross would pull Hans aside and they would walk together to the field, providing Hans a chance to share. I'll never forget the small acts of caring that individuals exhibited on our behalf.

During those weeks after Kjrsten's life was cut short, Hans' days at school were filled with classes and football even as he grieved for his sister. As a class assignment, Hans was asked to write a sestina-type poem in the style of the fixed verse form (the first stanza is used as line endings in each of the following stanzas). His "I AM" expresses the deep underlying sadness he was experiencing:

"I AM" POEM
Hans Hoeksema

I am funny and smart.
I wonder how the dinosauers died.
I hear doochy doochy.
I see a faun.
I want $1,000,000,000,000
I am funny and smart.

I pretend to be a knight.
I feel fire.
I touch a golden sea.
I worry about life.
I cry about death.
I am funny and smart.

I understand my parents.
I say Jesus Christ is Lord.
I dream about everything.
I try to be a good lineman.
I hope I see Kjrsten again.
I am funny and smart.

Friday morning we received a phone call from the Life Skills teacher at Baxter, Mrs. Karen Knapp. Karen was a fellow believer who had been at Kjrsten's funeral with many of Kjrsten's classmates. Karen was concerned and shared her concerns with us.

"The kids are asking lots of questions about what you said at Kjrsten's funeral—life, death, eternal life. And we are quite frankly not able to deal with much of it at school." I told Karen that we too were concerned about the kids but not sure what she was asking of us. Karen simply said she wanted us to know that Kjrsten's funeral had stirred up a great deal of interest in spiritual issues in the minds of many Baxter students. I thanked her and told her we'd do what we always did, 'We'd pray about it.'

Ardeth and I discussed Karen's concerns and prayed about whether this was an opportunity the Lord was directing. We concluded that if there were youth who wanted to talk about Kjrsten and her faith, we would be willing to be a part of that discussion.

Ardeth and I visited the school on the following Monday and met with Karen and Kjrsten's volleyball coach Brook Byars and informed them that "if there are kids who have questions about what Kjrsten believed and want to know more about her faith, we would open our home Sunday night October 3rd, and the kids were welcome to come and ask their questions." Ardeth drew up several small posters for Karen and Brook to post in their classrooms, and they put the word out at school.

✳✳✳

At 6:30 pm Sunday night the cars started arriving, bringing more than 20 high school kids to our home. We were shocked again. We thought perhaps 4 or 5 might want to talk things through but never imagined anything of this magnitude. Kjrsten's death had awakened a deep sense of spiritual questioning and searching in the minds of many young people in Baxter.

Our desire to work with youth is what initially drew Ardeth and me to each other. Living in Milwaukee at that time, we met while serving together on youth projects at the small Wesleyan Church we attended. Ardeth and I continued to be active with youth ministries at our church in Minnesota. We loved working with youth and felt blessed to have been given those opportunities in the past.

As Kjrsten's friends and classmates entered our home that evening, we began to realize all those years of youth work were likely part of God's plan to prepare us for this ministry. But we were absolutely floored that there were so many young people looking for answers. We had a large open great room in the basement, so the following week we ordered a pool table and a foosball table and began preparing for the next eight years of our ministry with the Baxter area youth.

We opened each session with prayer and the single guideline we have always used. We assured the youth, "We will answer everything we can, and we will defend it with Scripture. Because if it doesn't have the power of God's Holy Word behind it, it's simply another man's opinion." With that brief introduction, we outlined God's plan of salvation: How He sent His one and only son to die for our sins that we may be saved. We talked about what it meant to make a decision to accept Jesus Christ as your Lord and Savior.

I remember one question in particular. One of the young men in Kjrsten's class asked, "So if I accept Jesus, will everything be good?" His question wasn't quite clear to me and I asked him for clarification. He said "What I mean is, will good things happen to me?" Sam had had a difficult life already and was honestly asking if there were some tangible benefits to following Christ. I put my arm around his shoulder and told him, "Sam, if that were true, you and I wouldn't be having this conversation tonight."

That was the beginning of one of the greatest blessings God gave us in the aftermath of losing Kjrsten. For nearly eight years now, we have continued to meet nearly every Sunday night at 6:30 pm with youth from the Baxter area. The original intent was to make it for high school youth, but from the very beginning, the older youth would bring their younger siblings. So on any given Sunday night, 15–30 junior and senior high youth would gather for food, fun, fellowship and a look into God's Holy Word. That was the one thing that was, and still is, non-negotiable. We defend everything with Scripture.

Our church in Bondurant blessed us with the gift of 30 copies of the New International Version of the Bible that we continue to use every Sunday night. Watching a teenager look for a Scripture verse or passage and read it aloud is an amazing joy and privilege.

✳✳✳

But not everyone was pleased with what the Lord was doing through the tragedy. A few nights later I had a terrifying nightmare. Satan was standing at the end of the bed and looking right at me. He sneered and said just three short words, "I have her." I was shaking, scared. But I knew where Kjrsten was. I couldn't tell Ardeth about the nightmare, knowing how badly it would hurt. I immediately started praying for God's peace. He gave me much more.

Later that week, I awoke in the middle of the night. I was overcome with the sound of voices singing hymns—all the old favorites I had grown up with. The music continued and the voices kept singing. I couldn't stop the singing (even if I had wanted to). The strains to *We are standing on holy ground and there are angels standing all around,* played on. I thought to myself if I am on holy ground, I should be on my knees. So I climbed out of bed, knelt by the bed and entered into worship with the singing continuing all around me.

Suddenly, I felt someone gently touch my elbow and lift me to my feet. He was wearing a white robe and had sandy brown hair and possessed an inexplicable gentleness. The singing had stopped and the next thing I knew, we were standing outside a stone wall with an arched gateway. We looked into the courtyard, and there was Kjrsten. She wore a simple white knee length dress and was gracefully dancing in the courtyard. She actually looked over to us with an expression of complete and utter peace and contentment. She never spoke a word but immediately I heard the verse from Psalm 100:4, "Enter his gates with thanksgiving and his courts with praise." And then it was over. I was back in my bedroom, still on my knees, and the music was gone. I glanced at the red neon numbers on the bedside clock. It was 3:30 am when I had climbed out of bed, and now it was 3:44 am.

By now I was sure I was losing my mind. The grief must have made me start hallucinating. I crawled back into bed and didn't say a word to Ardeth when I left for work a few hours later. My early morning meeting was with good friend Scott Brunscheen who at the time was serving as the executive director of the Salisbury House in Des Moines—a Tudor-style mansion fashioned after King's House in Salisbury, England.

As we concluded our meeting, Scott shared with me, "I had the strangest thing happen to me last night. I woke up in the middle of the night and was overwhelmed with the feeling that I was supposed to pray for you. When I am in bed and feel the need to pray, I usually stay in bed and rarely get out. When God woke me last night to pray for you, I got out of bed and was on my knees. I am sure it was the Holy Spirit, but I don't know why."

I very hesitantly asked him, "What time was this?" He answered, "3:30 am." I felt the chills start at the top of my skull and tingle down my back. I proceeded to share with Scott my bizarre and amazing experience between 3:30 am and 3:44 am. In chapter 12 of 2 Corinthians when he says, "And I know that this man—whether in the body or apart from the body I do not know—was caught up to paradise." I can relate.

What an amazing God we serve. Not only had He cared enough to show me that Kjrsten was with Him, He then chose to confirm it through a fellow brother in Christ. When I left Scott, I called Ardeth, unable to keep last night's miracle a secret from her. I wasn't losing my mind, and I wasn't hallucinating. God provided exactly what I needed when I needed it. Praise be to God!

I was reminded of this in the note written by Dave Luick (a friend from our Minnesota church family) on one of the yellow cards from the funeral service, "The God with the strength to start the world spinning will stop to comfort those He knows by name."

CHAPTER 9

LIGHT SHINING
IN THE DARKNESS

"Shall we accept good from God and not trouble?"
Job 2:10b

Living in the aftermath
Baxter, Iowa

In the weeks following Kjrsten's funeral, Ardeth, Hans and I struggled to adjust to our loss. Sitting down at the family dinner table was gut wrenching. There was no way we could ignore the 800-pound gorilla in the room—the empty fourth chair. It was so difficult to accept the emptiness we felt as we sat at the table with four chairs and only three people to fill them. Shortly after the tragic car crash that cut 14-year-old Kjrsten's life short, a seventh grade classmate of Hans wrote a poem expressing the students' feelings entitled:

"The Empty Chair"
Jill Goldsmith

1 empty chair beside me
1 broken heart shattered for she

2 freshmen embracing
2 distraught parents, never replacing
3 people in the crash
1 girl died in the mash
2 people made it alive
1 teen died last night
1 angel looking from above
A whole school looking for love
Even though time will heal
The empty chair beside me is real.

Or the daily reminder of our loss when it came time for Hans to leave for school. With her driver's school permit, Kjrsten had driven him to school every day and suddenly she was gone. Ardeth re-arranged her work schedule at Halbrook Excavating in Ankeny to begin driving Hans back and forth to school. Hans wouldn't have to ride the school bus.

One day as Ardeth was driving Hans to school on the route requiring them to drive past the cemetery where Kjrsten was buried, he exclaimed, "I'm never going to be an uncle!" How do you respond to that? Ardeth put a positive spin on it by calmly explaining, "While it is true you will not have any nieces or nephews on our side of the family, you can still be an uncle from your future wife's side of the family."

***

Meanwhile, the Iowa state trooper who had briefly visited us at the hospital made arrangements to come to our home to personally share the accident report. "I am sorry to tell you that the blood tests for the individual who was driving the truck who killed your daughter showed he had meth in his system. He was driving with a suspended license and carried no automobile insurance." I asked how someone gets away with even registering a vehicle with no insurance?

The trooper explained that drivers will obtain insurance long enough to get the vehicle registered and then cancel the policy. "It's cheaper to pay the fine for driving without insurance (if they get caught) than it is to pay the premiums."

"The driver has not been officially charged in the accident yet as we want to thoroughly complete the investigation, but charges will eventually be forthcoming." He again offered his sincerest condolences and said to contact him at any time if we had questions.

Several months after Kjrsten's death, the Boone County District Attorney called and asked to come visit us. We made arrangements, and he arrived at our home several days later to discuss the case against the young man who killed Kjrsten. The DA explained that he was deliberating on which class of Vehicular Homicide to charge Brian. I asked, "What is the difference?" The DA explained that Class A involved controlled substances and carried a penalty up to 20 years while Class B did not involve controlled substances and carried up to a 10 year sentence.

"How do you want me to proceed?" he asked. The lab tests taken the night of the accident indicated a combination of Meth and prescription pain killers in Brian's system. "If there were narcotics in his system, then he should be charged with the Class A," I responded. The judicial system is never quite so black and white. "You need to know that Brian's attorney has filed a petition with the judge to have the blood test results thrown out, saying the troopers had no right to demand a blood sample that night."

I thought to myself, you have got to be kidding me. There was a horrific traffic fatality, and the police don't have the right to see if the driver was under the influence. This is ridiculous!

The DA thanked us for our time and said he'd let us know what his decision would be. Two days later we received a very short letter in the mail from the DA. "I know you won't agree with this decision, but I have agreed to a plea bargain that will include a Class B Vehicular Homicide conviction." Brian was sentenced to ten years at the Newton Correctional Facility and released in a little over three years.

✳✳✳

Before the sentencing, the judge sent us a questionnaire that included the opportunity to provide an 'impact statement' for his consideration before sentencing.

In response to Question #3—did you suffer any adverse change in your personal welfare or family relations as a result of this offense? If so, please describe. Ardeth wrote the following:

There were four of us and now there are three. We truly felt the four of us was "Heaven on Earth." Being together was the highlight of our day. The numbers are no longer equal and the hole left behind is deep and wide. The hole cannot be filled and that is what hurts, because the only thing that can fill it is not possible; Kjrsten back.

David and I made the decision that I should quit my job to be home with our son, Hans, for the summer. We didn't feel it would be good for any of us knowing he would be totally alone at home, even for the 3 days I worked. It was an easy decision because it is the best. However, I had a great job, good pay and loved it very much. I expect I will look for new employment in the fall when Hans heads back to school.

There are days David struggles to go to work. His greatest desire is to be with Hans and me. He worries about us and how we are doing. He is very protective and wants to "protect" us, even if it is just being with us.

Kjrsten was my first born, my only daughter and my very best girlfriend. We shared dreams and sorrows. I was her sounding board. The emotions and hurt cannot be described. I do not believe even Webster could do justice.

I have lost my shopping partner and the one who would share the appreciation of the "pretty" and "feminine" things in life. I walk into stores and refuse to look at all the "young girl" clothing, which is always at the front, in order for me to be able to function. I have had to leave stores in tears because I couldn't get past the front of the store.

I have lost one high school graduation, one college graduation, an engagement, a wedding, watching my best friend and husband escort my "baby girl" down the aisle, my only son-in-law and half of my grandchildren. In addition to those "big" events, I will miss every detail that goes with those and much more. This is all cut, dried and simple. And yet, everyone knows each one of these holds memories never to be shared or discovered.

There is always one missing at our table. And her brother still struggles with being "an only child." He has shared with us his loss of not being an "uncle" to his sister's children. We have shared with him that it is still possible through his wife's family. Some may think talking of grandchildren is odd, but Kjrsten's dream was to "bring her kids out to Grandpa and Grandma's to share what she loved." Her words, not ours. At only 13, her brother still sleeps on the couch outside our room, rather than in the basement where their bedrooms were close. He has bad dreams about not being able to save her. He will always miss her. She encouraged him and gave advice as he was struggling to figure out junior high school.

I have been given a life sentence without my daughter and she was exceptional in every way. I truly wish you could have met her, I'm sure you would have enjoyed the experience.

We loved her and love her still. We miss her and the joy she brought into our lives. We struggle because it seems that there are days the only way we can function is to consciously forget she existed. What parent does that? It is contrary to everything we believe and have done over the last 15 years.

In our old age, we were certain she would have been a caretaker of us with her brother. Now as time goes on, he will have sole responsibility. For even that I weep.

I ask Brian (last name withheld) to please take care of the life he has been given. Please do not waste the rest of your life. Consider this event and the loss and tragedy it is. Please make better choices. Every life has value and purpose. You have value and purpose.

As difficult as it is for me, it is important that I forgive you so I may continue my life without bitterness and with purpose. God is very clear in this regard. I live on with hope in my faith and the assurance of where my Kjrsten is. I will see her one day again, I know this. I do forgive you Brian.

Sincerely,
Ardeth Hoeksema, mother to Kjrsten Hoeksema

We were invited to the sentencing hearing scheduled for June 20, 2005, but opted not to attend. That was not the way I wanted to spend my 42nd birthday.

I struggled greatly with my feelings about Brian (last name withheld). On one hand I wanted somewhere, someone, to direct my anger towards—demanding that he suffer as I was suffering. On the other, I couldn't bring myself to hate him and God provided the peace to forgive him for which I am eternally thankful.

Several months later, we received a letter from Brian while he was still incarcerated. It was a genuine, heartfelt, deeply personal letter that I appreciated immensely. In corresponding back to Brian, I assured him that as Christ had forgiven us, we forgave him. But I also encouraged him to use this tragedy to move forward positively with his life with good decisions. Our prayer was that through this event, he too would come to know the Lord.

Living with the daily reminders of losing Kjrsten proved to be a very heavy burden for the three of us for years to come. At the beginning of his junior year in high school, Hans approached us with the news that he wanted to transfer from Baxter to Bondurant. When we pressed him as to why, he answered, "I struggle every day when I drive into town and have to drive by the cemetery and see Kjrsten's grave. I struggle every day when I have lunch in the cafeteria and look out at the courtyard at school dedicated to her memory. I struggle when young kids see Krjsten's picture on the wall in the cafeteria and want to know 'who is she.' There are just too many painful reminders here."

I pointed out that we can't run from our memories. He simply replied, "I understand that, but I don't have to have them smack me in the face every day that I'm in school either."

Looking back, the hurt and struggle Hans wrestled with daily was gruesome. The anniversary of Kjrsten's death was exceptionally difficult, most times resulting in Hans coming home from school early. Several years later while a sophomore at the University of Northern Iowa, Hans headed off to an early morning class. Halfway across campus he realized it was September 16th—the anniversary of Kjrsten's death. This time, wracked with guilt over 'how could I forget her?' he became physically ill and went to the campus clinic. After visiting with the physician, she told him, "Hans, you need to talk with someone" and referred him to a counselor.

A few weeks after that physician's referral, Hans and I were sharing dinner in Cedar Falls, and I asked him, "How's it going with the counseling?" In his very typical forthright manner, Hans answered, "I think we're done. We've hit bedrock." He proceeded to share that he felt cheated—that he lost his childhood at age 13. At a time when other kids were experiencing their usual teenage growing up years, Hans had felt as though he had to be responsible and care for his parents.

***

After Kjrsten's funeral, we didn't live day by day, we lived minute by minute. Slowly we stretched to hour by hour, and finally day by day. To think beyond that, to dream of the future was still too painful—always tempered by the reality of a future without Kjrsten.

Each day reiterated what our changed reality meant. The ever present wonderings existed about the 'what ifs' and 'what might have beens.' We would never see Kjrsten graduate from college. I would never get to walk her down the aisle on her wedding day. How many grandchildren had I lost?

With my mind still reeling from the enormity of the loss, I found myself asking lots of questions. Friends and associates were always ready with pat answers like "God is good" and "Nothing happens without a reason." I started looking closer at the 'sound bites' people used to try and make us feel better about our loss. What I realized was that they (and we) were omitting key parts of the promises of Scripture. True, God is good. But the remainder of the verse explains how—because "His love endures forever." Not because 'only good things will happen to me.' Somewhere down the road of my distant past, I had bought into the premise that only good will come from the hand of God. In a paraphrase of verse, 2:10B, Job said it well when rebuking his wife after the loss of their children, "Should I only expect good from the hand of God and not bad as well?"

Even Jesus said in John 16:33, "In this world you will have trouble, but take heart; for I have overcome the world."

✳✳✳

Our entire story of loss and grief finally meshed for me as God revealed the following analogy. When Kjrsten accepted Christ as her Lord and Savior, she definitely became His, and not mine. She and I were brothers and sisters in Christ at that point. The apostle Paul in his second letter to Timothy instructed him in verse 3 to "endure hardship with us like a good soldier of Jesus Christ." We are soldiers in His service. There are battlefield commanders who regularly must order troops to fulfill a mission. Obeying a command of, "You three go charge that pillbox," is a suicide mission, but none the less, one that has to be carried out. The commander gains no sense of pleasure in sending those soldiers on that mission recognizing they may very well not be coming back. However, the greater good of the unit demands the sacrifice.

Jesus sent Kjrsten on a mission that was important to Him. Nothing more—nothing less.

As I sat in my home office early one morning, I remembered something Ken Cook had told me at the visitation the evening before Kjrsten's funeral. Ken and Evelyn Cook were a farm family in New Providence, Iowa. Their youngest daughter Sheryl, who was a year behind me in school, had been killed just out of high school in a tragic accident involving a snow plow, limited visibility and icy winter roads. I asked Ken, "How did you get over that?" Ken told me something that we can now attest to as well, "You never get over it; you just get better at carrying the pain."

Now I sat wondering "how long does the pain last? How long will it take to feel some sense of healing? How long before I want to live again?" Because the truth was, at that point, I didn't. The pain of losing a child is impossible to describe. There isn't even a name for it. The loss of parents—an orphan. The loss of a spouse—a widow or widower. The loss of a child—simply no category to fill the void.

There were times when the enormity of the loss literally took my breath away. I felt I couldn't catch my breath. There was a physical pain that felt like an anvil sitting on my chest. There were times when the tears just flowed, and I could not stop them. And then there were other times when I just couldn't believe it was happening. Not to us—perhaps to others—but not to us. Some friends of ours from Minnesota lost their daughter suddenly to meningitis years ago. (Their daughter had been in our high school Sunday school class.) After Kjrsten was killed, they sent us a very kind letter. In it they shared with us how the loss of their child had propelled them into active roles in the church that they would not have otherwise pursued.

Ardeth and I were already active in church and ministry. We had served the Lord our entire adult lives. We loved God and offered Him our time, talent and treasure to the best of our ability. And we had carefully and proactively instilled these same Kingdom priorities in our children. So why us? There it was again. The 'whys' continued creeping into our thoughts. Why Kjrsten, God? If someone needed rescuing, why not the abused and abandoned child — that would at least have been a blessing. And why Ardeth and me? Hadn't we always been faithful to do whatever we heard you asking from us?

✳✳✳

Once again, the answer to our questioning is found in God's Word. Contemporary writer Eugene H. Peterson in his paraphrase of the Old Testament 'Introduction to Job,' writes

"It is not only because Job suffered that he is important to us. It is because he suffered in the same ways that we suffer—in vital areas of family, personal health, and material things. Job is also important to us because he searchingly questioned and boldly protested his suffering. Indeed, he went 'to the top' with his questions.

It is not the suffering that troubles us. It is undeserved suffering. Almost all of us in our years of growing up have had the experience of disobeying our parents and being punished for it. When that discipline was connected with wrongdoing, it had a certain sense of justice to it: When we do wrong, we get punished.

One of the surprises as we grow older, however, is that we come to see that there is no real correlation between how much wrong we commit and the subsequent pain we experience. An even greater surprise is that very often there is something quite the opposite: We do right and get knocked down. We strive to do our very best, and just as we are reaching out to receive our reward we are blindsided and sent reeling."

Yeah, that's exactly what I was thinking. One particular afternoon as I stopped at the mailbox on the rural highway at the end of our half-mile gravel driveway, I looked to the sky and yelled at God at the top of my lungs. No audible words were necessary—it was just the raging of a father who knew his world was shattered. My heart was broken, and I wanted to make sure He knew it.

✳✳✳

It was at this point a dear friend, Dave Bertsch gave me a book authored by Charles (Chuck) Swindoll. While Ardeth and I were living in Minnesota, I was blessed to be part of a men's group that met for several years. We would gather before work for breakfast or after work for dessert or in one of our homes on Saturday morning—whatever it took to accommodate busy work schedules my travel schedule and the demands of families with young children. All four of these brothers in Christ attended Kjrsten's funeral—David Bertsch, Brooks Larson, Steve Eddy and Tim Schmitz.

The book was simply titled 'Job-A Man of Heroic Endurance.' It was a hand-autographed hard copy that Pastor Swindoll had given Dave and he was passing it on to me. The book's dedication had a profound impact on me:

"This book is dedicated to all in the family of God
who are going through times of great suffering
and have been devastated by the pain you have had to endure.

Like Job, you have been unable to understand why.
Like Job, you have not deserved the affliction,
but the pain continues.
Like Job, you have prayed for answers
and waited for God to bring relief.
Neither has occurred.

Like Job, you keep praying and waiting.
Like Job, you sometimes wonder, "Where is God?"
He remains silent and seems aloof.
Nevertheless, you faithfully endure.
Because of that, like Job, you will someday be greatly rewarded.
You have my highest admiration."

Wow. That really summed up how we were feeling. At those darkest times— where was God?

Swindoll opens the first chapter of the book with this:

"Life is difficult. That blunt, three-word statement is an accurate appraisal of our existence on this planet. When the writer of the biblical book named Job picked up his stylus to write his story, he could have begun with a similar-sounding and equally blunt sentence, 'Life is unfair.'"

Swindoll goes on to explain that *"There are trials we endure we do not deserve, but they are permitted. You read that correctly. Life includes trials that we do not deserve, but they must, nevertheless, be endured.*

In the mystery of God's unfathomable will, we can never explain or fully understand. Do not try to grasp each thread of His profound plan. If you resist my counsel here, you'll become increasingly more confused, ultimately resentful, and finally bitter. At that point, Satan will have won the day. Accept it. Endure the trial that has been permitted by God. Nothing touches your life that has not first passed through the hands of God. He is in full control and because He is, He has the sovereign right to permit trials that we do not deserve."

For the first time since my questioning began, I finally had the answer. And the answer was, "quit asking." Job finally recognized that as well.

Job lost his children too. But he still found in the depths of his faith the wisdom to utter the words, "Shall we accept good from God, and not trouble? The Lord gave and the Lord has taken away; may the name of the Lord be praised." God gave, and for some unrevealed reason, He chose to take Kjrsten back. She was always His—it's ALL His.

The formal grieving had to end. Hans had returned to school two days later; I had to get back to work but Ardeth endured the most difficult challenge. Working part-time outside the home, she was left with too many hours alone in an empty house with only her memories to occupy her time.

How does one 'go on living' when a part of your life has been violently taken away? Ardeth and I were conscious of the need to give Hans as normal (whatever that meant now?) a life as possible. The first fork in the road came soon after Kjrsten's death.

We had planned a trip to Rome for Thanksgiving that year. Ironically, it was a trip that Kjrsten had selected and helped to plan. As she was the oldest sibling, this year it was her turn to choose where she would like the family to visit. It was to be a fantastic getaway with my brother John and his wife Regina. As my family loved history, this was to be a very special trip.

What do you do now? Go or not go? So we sat down with Hans and asked him, "what would you like to do?" "I still want to go" he said.

So we did. And while we recognize many things have obviously been different than they would have been had Kjrsten lived, we have diligently tried to continue living life to the fullest—again with no regrets.

One of God's great supports and encouragements in the weeks, months and years to follow Kjrsten's death was music —specifically contemporary Christian music. We had been faithful listeners of KNWI 107.1 FM since their arrival in Des Moines. But their ministry in music was very personal now. It was uncanny how at innumerable times they would play a song whose words spoke to my heart as if divinely appointed at that precise hour (which I am sure they were).

One of the great fears of a parent who has lost a child is that their son or daughter will be forgotten. And we seek opportunities to keep their memory alive. One of the ways for us was to sponsor a 'day of listening' on the radio for both Han's and Kjrsten's birthdays. We had always appreciated the positive alternative music that KNWI provided for our children and were blessed that they both loved the music.

Sponsoring Christian music on the radio is a tradition we still keep every year—honoring our children and their right choices and helping support another of Christ's ministries.

***

Ardeth and I were amazed by the outpouring of memorial support given in Kjrsten's honor. We received over $10,000 from friends, family and even strangers. Now we were faced with what to do with the money. We knew we would not keep it for ourselves, and we didn't want to use it for her funeral. We wanted to find a lasting tribute to Kjrsten and to her life. Something for which she would be remembered.

Since 1998, I had the privilege of traveling to Mexico nearly every winter with a group of other men to help build churches. The annual trips began while we were involved with Trinity Evangelical Free Church in Lakeville, Minnesota, and now continued with Bondurant Federated Church. During any given year, 12 to 15 men would pack up and head for Iquala located in the State of Guerro, Mexico.

At the time we were working with missionary Paul Stilwell, serving with Missions to Latin America who hosted work teams from the United States throughout the winter months.

Paul's philosophy and mission was to work with villages and towns where there were Christians already meeting regularly for worship. After finding a way to acquire land and building the shell of a church, Paul would partner a work team from the United States with the local church to finish the project by completing the roof. The work teams provided the cash for the concrete roofing materials and some of the labor.

Those trips were some of my best memories that I still cherish. The Mexican brothers and sisters were so gracious and loving to their 'gringo' brothers from America. Our task was typically to help pour concrete roofs for small rural churches. We would normally spend two or three days setting up for the pour. Unlike completing such a task in the United States where a hardware store is around the corner, we were in isolated villages, often without electricity, and with very little in the way of building materials and tools. The Lord always provided a way. Using wire instead of nails to cobble together support beams and clear plastic hoses filled with water for levels, it always came together.

In one particularly remote location, all the steel rebar, all the sand, all the gravel, all the cement, and all the water for the concrete roof had to be hauled up the last mile of the mountain using burros. Sleeping on the ground or on planks around the work site while establishing lasting relationships with brothers in Christ was incredibly special. And when I returned home after each year's mission trip and shared the stories, Kjrsten more than Ardeth or Hans, would get so excited. "When can I go Dad? I want to go." Our plan was to make that happen someday with a family work project to Mexico.

A highlight of each year's trip was the worship service. We would gather with the local church fellowship for Sunday evening worship. Paul would normally ask Pastor Jeff to preach. However, Jeff speaks no Spanish, so Paul would interpret. On one occasion, Jeff preached in English, Paul translated into Spanish, and the local lay church leader had to interpret into Mistico, the local Indian dialect of the village. Most years, the hymns and praise songs were in Spanish, a language none of us knew. But we could occasionally recognize the tune and we'd sing in English or more often just hum along.

✳✳✳

In January, 2005, our church from Bondurant was again taking a team back to work with Paul in Iguala. After having just recently lost Kjrsten I had decided that this would be the first year that I would not be part of the team. I needed to be home with my family. Ardeth challenged me, "While our lives have changed and not for the better, we still need to do what we did before Kjrsten died. And that includes service. You need to go."

The more we discussed it, the more I realized she was right. And as we continued to talk about the upcoming missions trip, we fondly recalled Kjrsten's desire to be a part of missions work. We also knew through Paul's mission newsletter that his fifteen-passenger van was past its last leg.

We decided it would be a fitting way to remember Kjrsten—to help purchase a van in her honor to be used for the glory of God—carting work teams and missionaries around Mexico. We made arrangements to wire Paul the money, so he could purchase the van.

Just a few weeks after Kjrsten's funeral, on October 26, 2004, we received an email from Paul.

"Thank you for the memorial money, Dave and Ardeth. I don't know what you think about modern-day prophecy, but I wanted to share something that happened. This summer on our trip a friend stopped me at a church in Ridgeland, Wisconsin, and said something like 'I feel like the Lord wants me to tell you that the remainder of the funds for the van purchase will be provided in a very special and unexpected way.' I take words from the Lord like that with a grain of salt, but I sincerely believe now that God was speaking to me through my friend about Kjrsten and your family and that he was saying then that you are very special to Him, just as you continue to be today. We will plan to use the memorial money for the van, and we should be able to make the purchase within a couple weeks."

That year when our team arrived, Pastor Jeff brought along a small engraved brass plaque that he attached to the dash board of the van. It simply read:

In Memory of Kjrsten Hoeksema
Taking God's love and salvation to the ends of the earth
Acts 1:8

Kjrsten didn't travel to Mexico on a work team. But for each of the past seven years she has helped transport 8 to 10 missionary teams (annually, each with 10 to 15 volunteers). My math makes that nearly 1,000 mini-missionaries she rode along with throughout Mexico. Not bad. Of the memorial funds, Paul needed $8,000 to purchase the van and the balance was used to establish the Kjrsten Hoeksema Memorial Fund at our church providing scholarships for youth to attend summer mission trips.

✳✳✳

But we also had an overwhelming, pressing need to remember Kjrsten locally. So in the spring of 2005, I visited with long-time Baxter School Superintendent Neil Seales. As is typically the case in small town schools, Neil was more than just the superintendent. He was the high school track coach with an excellent record of highly competitive and winning teams. Even when in his late forties, Neil would still get out and run with the teams. And in many cases, he could still win.

I always believed Neil loved his job because he was devoted to the kids. Visiting with Neil that day was very difficult for both of us. Not only was he the school administrator, but his daughter Katie had been a friend and classmate of Kjrsten's. Small towns are like big families, and they had just lost one of their own. We talked briefly about how the students and staff were dealing with the loss—after all it had only been a few months since the accident. Then, I shared with Neil my purpose for being there. "Neil, we want to do something to remember Kjrsten and would like to do something for the school at the same time. Is there anything that you need?"

Neil and I came up with just the thing. The school in Baxter is reminiscent of small towns with one building for grades kindergarten through 12th grade. Our school was fighting the trends in Iowa of consolidation and larger school districts and had recently built a new addition to the school. Neil was once again the local hero having written a successful grant that provided a significant portion of the funding for the expansion. I accompanied him on a quick tour, and we stopped at the point where the new addition joined the old facility. The completed construction project had left a 36′ by 120′ open air enclosure. According to Neil, future plans called for turning it into a courtyard suitable for outdoor classroom use.

It seemed like an ideal way to remember Kjrsten. She loved school. She loved to read. And Baxter had been a good fit for Kjrsten—she had excelled here.

What better way to honor her than in creating a space for generations of young students to enjoy?

Working with a local landscape designer, Cindy Foreman, we created a beautiful garden with a concrete flagstone walkway, trees and shrubs, rock waterway, Victorian era streetlights complete with wrought iron benches for reading. When completed, it was named 'Kit's Courtyard'. Cindy donated the bulk of her time and that of her crew to help construct the project. She later shared with Ardeth and me an encounter she'd had with Kjrsten the summer before. When we built our home in the country, we had hired Cindy to do our landscaping design and installation. During one of her trips to the house while she and the crew were at work, Kjrsten had gone outside to just visit with them. Cindy recalled how much that gesture meant because so often they're ignored on the job site. But not by Kjrsten. She loved people. For that matter, she just loved life.

The other task that weighed heavily on us during those months after Krjsten's death, was securing a suitable head stone for her grave. We were troubled by not having a permanent marker in place. Even without a head stone, students were regularly visiting her grave, often leaving small tokens—notes, trinkets, pictures—of their enduring friendship.

We were convinced that her headstone needed to clearly point people to Jesus Christ because that is what Kjrsten would have wanted. She had a very real burden for her friends' salvation and talked to us frequently about it. For the inscription on the front of the headstone was her name, date of birth, class year and 'beloved daughter, treasured sister and faithful friend.' On the back, we finally settled on Romans 10:9: 'If you confess with your mouth and believe in your heart that Jesus is Lord, you will be saved.' We wanted any and every visitor to the gravesite to know how to receive the gift of eternal life and to remind them that Kjrsten was in Heaven. On that same side of the monument we added 'I'm laughing, dancing, and singing praises to my Lord; I look forward to the day when we are re-united in Heaven.'

Kjrsten's time here on earth may have been cut short, but her ministry was just beginning.

CHAPTER 10

MERCIES IN DISGUISE

Peace I leave with you; my peace I give you.
I do not give to you as the world gives. Do not let your
hearts be troubled and do not be afraid.
John 14:27

2005–2012
Baxter, Iowa

The Lord continued to 'make a way' for us. It was never easy. I judged my healing progress by how much I still cried. It seemed I cried nearly as often, but the spells became shorter. Ken Cook was correct, "you never did get over the pain, you just got better at carrying it."

We obviously did a great deal of soul searching those first few years after Kjrsten was killed. And over time, God began to reveal things that were always there but never in focus. Looking back and clearly seeing the hand of God preparing us not just to endure such an event but truly thrive was both amazing and humbling.

• God told me the morning Kjrsten was born as I drove home from the hospital, "David, someday you will have to give her away."

• God already saved Kjrsten once and gave us nearly 15 wonderful years with a perfectly healthy, beautiful, smart, wonderful girl when we could have lost her before she was even born when she suffered the stroke that created the void in her brain.

• God allowed us to have a clean conscious as we told the doctors and nurses to "let her go" that night in the emergency room because four days earlier Kjrsten told us at the kitchen counter, "If anything happens to me, and I'm going to be a vegetable, let me go. I'll just get there before you do." God allowed us to say goodbye with No Regrets.

• God put a song of rejoicing in our hearts even in the midst of life's tragedy as we sang praises in the van heading home that dreadful night.

• God refused to allow Satan to steal our peace and sent His angel to show us Kjrsten alive and rejoicing in Heaven.

• God allowed Kjrsten to tell us goodbye in her own handwriting etched in the margins of her day planner the very day she was killed through the lyrics of Collin Raye's 'Love, Me': *If you get there before I do.*

• God allowed us to watch Kjrsten walk across the stage and receive an award at Iowa State University as part of her Talented and Gifted student program. (In lieu of seeing her college graduation.)

• God gave us a 'peace that passes understanding' (John 14:27) and never allowed us to hate Brian or end up as bitter and angry people.

• God allowed Kjrsten to have a great impact in Mexico missions—a desire of her heart. In the summer after her death, the Baxter Area Youth group's first annual mission's trip was to Mexico to work with missionary Paul Stilwell.

• God preserved a close and loving relationship between Ardeth and me when statistically 80 percent of marriages that suffer the loss of a child end in divorce. Dr. Trent penned it well in his book, 'The Blessing': *As a marriage counselor, time and again I've seen one spouse (or both) take a step away from the other when challenges come up. When they do this, something starts dying in their relationship. The more they move away from each other, the more problematical their marriage becomes. So that's the life-or-death choice when it comes to relationships. At any given juncture we make the choice to move toward the other person, choosing life in that relationship, or to step away, choosing death."* We chose LIFE!

• God raised our son Hans to be a young man of great faith and conviction, filled with joy—not anger and resentment.

• God gave us the strength to focus our love to our only remaining child, Hans, without holding him too tightly in fear.

• God prepared us for youth ministry years in advance that we might serve the youth of the Baxter community.

• Most importantly, God not only saved our faith, He grew our faith.

***

Over time, I kept looking for the kingdom secrets I felt God had told me He would show me as we struggled through the healing process.

1. I now realize in crystal clear clarity that this world is not my home.

I had always known heaven awaited those who love the Lord, but I never understood until now that Heaven wasn't a side dish for when this earthly existence was over. Rather, it is the main course. Being reunited with our heavenly Father is what we were created for. For the first time, I found myself filled with a sense of excitement and anticipation about the promise of eternal life. Someday I was going home, and it wasn't to Baxter.

Randy Alcorn wrote an amazing in-depth thesis on eternity—simply titled 'Heaven.' It was only a matter of months after Kjrsten was killed that I was introduced to his work. After reading his book, for the first time I longed for Heaven. He completely transformed my ideal heaven. I was excited to be there.

2. I now have a much keener understanding that my only hope lies in Jesus Christ. Nothing I can do or control will ever provide the security, joy and peace

that comes from Him. He promises us a "peace that passes understanding."

On a particular Sunday morning as I sat in the same pew we always did, I was battling with the feelings that God could have stopped the tragedy. If He really loved me, why didn't He prevent the accident? And then He gave me the mental picture of a man stranded on a rock in the crashing ocean surf. The night before his ship had crashed on the same rock in a terrible storm. Now he clung to that rock for his very survival.

That was an illustration of how I felt. God could have prevented the crash but in His sovereignty, He chose not to. But my only hope for surviving the tragedy was to cling to Him like the sailor clinging to the rock that sunk his ship.

3. **I now have a much greater personal appreciation for what Jesus has done for me.**

Another change happened in my heart. As depicted throughout this book, for Ardeth and me, church has been an important part of our lives since we were young children. After all, we were both PKs (preacher's kids) and had grown up in the church. But through this ordeal, God had sensitized my heart and being in church was turning out to be a very emotional roller coaster. Oftentimes, just uttering the precious name of Jesus was enough to bring me to tears. I now had a much greater sense of appreciation for the personal sacrifice He made for me. After all, I knew for a fact that He had saved my daughter for eternity. I had so much to be thankful for.

Soon after Kjrsten was killed, someone told me,

"Remember you have a God who knows what it's like to lose a child." And my less than kind retort was "Tell me I get Kjrsten back in three days and I'm fine with it." But months later while sitting in church and still thinking about that concept, out of the blue God spoke to me again saying "David, but think of the millions I never get back."

I just cried and asked for forgiveness. God, please forgive the ramblings of a fool. I know not of what I speak. I lost a child who was technically His to begin with. He's losing thousands everyday—and losing them for eternity.

4. **I now recognize that God indeed has a plan for my life. It is not a series of random occurrences but individual experiences brought together by the Conductor of the Universe.**

Ardeth and I have been so blessed, and we tried very hard to stay focused on the blessings and not the hurt. I used a jigsaw puzzle as an object lesson with the youth group one Sunday night. I held up two or three pieces of the puzzle that were dark and black with no appeal whatsoever. "If these pieces represent your life, what does it look like to you?" The responses were exactly what you'd expect. "Ugly" "Depressing" "Boring" "No joy" etc. But then I unveiled the cover of the box that depicted the completed puzzle as a dazzling bouquet of flowers. Rich and vibrant colors of bright reds, yellows, orange and blue blended together in a beautiful tapestry.

"If we only view our life in the context of one or two dark pieces, like losing Kjrsten, we can see our lives as terrible mistakes. But when we see what God sees, which is the whole picture, He has a wonderful plan for our lives. In Jeremiah He says, "I have a plan for you; a plan to prosper you." There will be painful pieces in our jigsaw puzzle of life, but our hope is in seeing His completed purpose. When He places the final piece in our puzzle, and we see what beautiful things He had in store for us, we will rejoice together in Heaven forever.

5. **I now fully understand that what I do in this life matters for all eternity.**

Bruce Wilkinson, wrote a wonderful book we have used extensively with our youth group entitled 'A Life God Rewards for Teens.' His book raises a very important question: Do you believe your choices today will have a direct impact on your life one million years from now? He suggests our eternal life is a line that has no end and our earthly life is a tiny dot on the line. His premise, with which I now concur, is that what happens "in the dot" greatly determines what happens "on the line." Even a small choice in the dot can have a huge, and eternal consequence, on the line.

Where we spend eternity is based on what we BELIEVE while here on earth; how we spend eternity is greatly influenced by our BEHAVIOR while here on earth. The crucial question is 'Are we living for the dot or living for the line?'

He shares the story of an English couple who were missionaries in some far off part of the world. It was in the early 1800s, so travel was slow and difficult. Consequently, they stayed abroad for many years. Finally, they wrote to their supporters back in England to let them know they were coming home. After a lengthy voyage, they approached the English port.

The husband asked his wife, "Do you suppose anyone will be waiting for us?" When they arrived at the dock, they were shocked to see the pier filled with a large crowd gathered behind a Welcome Home banner. "Wow," they said. "This is really great. We'd better go below deck and gather our bags." By the time they were ready to exit the ship, the crowd was gone. Turns out a prominent politician had already left the ship and the crowd vanished with him. The missionary turned to his wife, somewhat dejected and said, "After a lifetime of service, this isn't much of a welcome home."

"Come along sweetheart," she lovingly replied. "This is just England, we're not home yet."

6. **I'm not home 'til I'm with Jesus! That's the greatest kingdom secret God has shared with me.**

✳✳✳

Kjrsten was special. I realize coming from her father that observation has to be taken with a grain of salt. But Kjrsten's children's Musical Director, Deb Frandsen, obviously felt the same way. Deb approached us several months after Kjrsten's death with an idea. She wanted to create the 'Kit Award' using Kjrsten's nickname to recognize the individual child who exemplified the greatest service and leadership traits each year in the children's musical—traits that emulated Kjrsten's life. Each year our church honors one child who exhibits these characteristics with an inscribed plaque. Hard work, commitment, integrity, caring and compassion, service—that about sums up Kjrsten's attitude.

We stepped back into our role of teaching the junior and senior high school Sunday school at Bondurant Federated. And, we continued meeting with the Baxter Area Youth (now the name of the youth group) every Sunday night. Working with the youth was another of God's blessings in our lives.

***

And the Lord continued to provide opportunities to share our story dedicated to His glory. In May of 2005, Dr. Gary Rosberg invited us for an interview with his wife Barb on their syndicated radio show, "America's Family Coaches."

(To listen to the interview, visit our website at www.MissionHillIowa.com).

In 2006, Mark Tauchek, the reporter for WHO–TV in Des Moines who initially contacted Ardeth, and asked if she was still connecting with any of Kjrsten's friends. "Funny you should ask. We see many of them every Sunday night," Ardeth replied. Ardeth had shared with Mark about the youth group in previous conversations when Mark had followed-up to just 'check on how we were doing.' As Ardeth shared how it was still going strong, Mark asked if we were open to letting him do a story on the youth group. He explained that they were compiling a series called 'Hearts of Gold'—a complement to the Olympics comprised of 10 segments featuring heart-warming human interest stories. We told him it was fine with us, but the decision belonged to the youth as it was their group, we were just facilitators.

That Sunday night Ardeth explained WHO-TV's concept for the story to the youth group kids and sought their input regarding Mark's request. The kids thought it was a great idea. So a few weeks later, Mark brought out a film crew and recorded that Sunday night's youth group gathering. It turned out to be another wonderful blessing, allowing us to share the good news of Jesus Christ with an even broader audience.

(To preview the WHO-TV 'Hearts of Gold' special, visit our website at www.MissionHillIowa.com)

***

There were many touching examples of people who cared. On the one year anniversary of Kjrsten's death, I took the day off and stayed home to be with my wife. We went into Baxter to visit Kjrsten's grave and then headed home. As we drove up our long lane, we saw a car that we didn't recognize and a man sitting on the front steps of house. It was Brooks Larson, one of my former Bible study buddies from Minneapolis, Minnesota. "I decided not to call because I was sure you'd tell me not to make the drive." I'll never forget that kind of dedicated compassion in action. You don't ask "Is there anything I can do for you?" Instead, you just do. As Yoda said, "Do, or do not. There is no try."

We had friends who would see us at church on Sundays and say "I was thinking about you this week and wanted to call but didn't want to disturb you." Guess what? Please disturb us. We need the distraction. Or they'd say "I was going to call but didn't know what to say and didn't want to make you feel bad." Again, guess what? There is nothing you can say to make us feel any worse than we already do.

If I could give advice (it's free so it may not be worth much), the one thing I would encourage readers to remember is that when you have the opportunity to show you care—don't hesitate. Just do it. Right then and there.

Or the time when a friend (who would prefer to remain anonymous) handed me a check for $1,000 at Kjrsten's memorial service and to this day continues to be a loyal and faithful brother in Christ.

Or the time when a former client (now friend from Ottawa, Illinois) made the long drive to come visit Ardeth and me. Luke and Kathy Caruso had lost a daughter of their own and understood the incredible pain and loss. They knew what we were struggling with and had maintained their faith through the storm. If my anchor doesn't hold during the storm, what good is it? Jesus held fast.

Or when three friends of Kjrsten's independently received tattoos with one word permanently engraved on their skin 'KIT.' (I have often pondered getting a tattoo myself but I could never decide what it would say.) And the friends who created the Facebook account in Kjrsten's honor that they continue to regularly update.

Years later, in 2012, Jenn Saak, one of Kjrsten's good friends and talented local artist (who found Kjrsten's promise ring in the bottom of her gym bag), created an art exhibit honoring Kjrsten. Jenn planned a series of oil paintings entitled *A Life of Sitting*. Jenn claims on Facebook, 'Kjrsten 100 percent inspired this series.' We continue to be blessed by phone calls, Facebook postings and the occasional visits from some of her classmates from Baxter.

God has been so gracious to Ardeth and me for nearly 30 years of marriage. I have an amazing and wonderful wife, a son who is now in his twenties and is himself a committed man of God whom I could not be more proud of, and I have the promise of eternity with my daughter and my sister in Christ in Heaven—not much to complain about.

We lived life to the fullest in our family and never missed an opportunity to share time together. We had been blessed to travel extensively as a family around the world—building wonderful lasting memories.

But sometimes the questions still pop-up in the back of my mind, 'God why?' I believe John Wesley provided the most appropriate answer when he wrote, "Bring me a worm that can comprehend a man and then I will show you a man that can comprehend the triune God."

EPILOGUE

I frequently am asked, "David, why did you write this book?" The simple answer is I just didn't want to forget. I didn't want to forget Kjrsten, her life, her beauty, her attitude, her smile. After eight years, memories fade and at times it feels like family photographs are all that's left.

But a more accurate answer would include the absolute conviction to share with others the great gifts that I believe God, through His son Jesus Christ, has shared with me. There is no question that we have suffered greatly through the loss of Kjrsten. But there is also no question that we have been greatly blessed as well.

God loves me. So much so that He gave His only son to die on the cross so that I could spend eternity with Him. He gave that same gift to Kjrsten for which I am eternally and profoundly grateful. And He has offered that same gift to you.

We do not know what tomorrow holds for any of us. Our lives, like Kjrsten's, can be cut short at any time. What's important is are we ready when that day arrives? Kjrsten was.

She had invited Jesus to be Lord of her life years ago. Have you? Are you ready should your life be demanded of you this day?

The original working title for the book was *No Regrets*. That title was a fitting reminder of how we have lived our lives as the Hoeksema family. It is true, I obviously regret that Kjrsten is not here with us. I regret that I didn't get to see her graduate from college this past May. I regret that I never got to walk her down the aisle on her wedding day. But I have No Regrets of the time we had with her. We lived life to the fullest at every opportunity possible, before and after losing her.

I would encourage you to do the same. Never miss an opportunity to tell your spouse or your children how much you love them, how proud you are of them, how special and important they are to you. Take every opportunity to spend time together, experiencing all the wonders—big and small— that God has given us. Live your life each day so that you can look back one day and simply realize "I have lived my life with No Regrets."

DAVID HOEKSEMA

As a child, David spent three years in East Africa as the son of a pastor and missionary, igniting a love for history and travel.

David and his wife, Ardeth, have been married for nearly 30 years. They attend an evangelical church and have served as deacon/deaconess, Sunday school and youth group teachers, led Bible studies and supported missions trips.

David is founder and president of Renaissance Group, Inc., Des Moines, Iowa, a fundraising consulting firm. He has served non-profit organizations across the United States in this capacity since 1983. He is a graduate of William Penn University.

David and Ardeth have two children—Hans, a college student and Kjrsten, who has been waiting to greet them at Heaven's Gate, since September 16, 2004.

ANSWERING THE CALL

It was in 1985 when I was an unmarried single guy working for Growth Design Corporation that I experienced a life-changing transformation despite my initial resistance to God's plan for my life. I was living in Milwaukee and loving my job—but not much involved with my church. I attended a large eastside church that allowed me to slide into a pew on Sunday morning, sit through the service, and just as quickly 'exit stage right' immediately afterward. Traveling a great deal on consulting business, I rationalized that my schedule prevented me from taking a more active role in my church.

My spiritual complacency was rudely interrupted when I began distinctly hearing the voice of the Holy Spirit calling me to ministry. Specifically, I felt I was being challenged to pursue the pastorate. While I greatly admired my father for his chosen vocation as a pastor and missionary and wished to be obedient to the Lord's desire for my own life, I was hugely conflicted. I truly enjoyed my consulting work, my clients and my colleagues.

The internal tug of war continued nonstop for nearly six months. I finally relented and yielded to God saying, "If you want me to enroll in seminary, fine; I'll go." As a result, in August of that same year I asked my childhood friend Scott Cook to use his private pilot's license and plane to fly me to Asbury, Kentucky, home of Asbury Theological Seminary—my father's alma mater—for student visitation weekend. I had the opportunity to tour the campus, visit with the faculty, and in two short days become genuinely excited about this new chapter unfolding in my life.

✷✷✷

On Sunday morning while walking across the campus with the admissions counselor, I informed him of my decision. "This is where I want to be. Go ahead and sign me up." "That's terrific," the counselor replied. "We're full for this semester, but in January you can register for second semester classes."

I was devastated. How could a private school afford to be "full" and turn prospective students away? I remember asking, "God, what are you doing? For six months you kept me in turmoil until I finally agree to do what you want me to do," and then I hear, 'I don't want you.'

And, in what was the closest thing to an audible conversation I've ever had with God, I heard Him say, "No, David. I do want you. And I wanted to know you'd do whatever I asked and you needed to know it too. Right now I want you in Milwaukee."

To me, that meant finding a place to actively serve God. I

was quite sure that's what He was urging me to do. So, after the weekend in Asbury, immediately upon my return to Milwaukee, I looked up Wesleyan Churches. I figured if their seminary was good, their churches must be too. There are several Wesleyan churches in Milwaukee, and I selected the one closest to the house where the owners had rented out the ground floor to me.

After calling the church office to determine worship times, I settled back and waited for Sunday to arrive. That Sunday morning I made my way across town to Trinity Wesleyan Church. Over the past decades the neighborhood had changed considerably and was now a very diverse area of Milwaukee.

The church building itself was extremely small and not in the least awe inspiring. I stopped my car on the street but didn't even pull into the parking lot. My conversation began again with the Holy Spirit. "This can't be possible. This isn't where I'm supposed to be," I announced as I pulled away from the curb. Before I had even driven one block past the church, I was convicted by the urging of the Holy Spirit to turn back and go inside. I turned right, then two more rights, and pulled into the church parking lot.

I approached the church doors with trepidation but also with a sense of mission. When I walked into church that day, Ardeth was leading the singing. Our romance was not a 'love at first sight' infatuation. I had felt led to that Wesleyan Church because God had something for me to do although when I saw the church I couldn't imagine what or how. But true to His promises, if we are willing, He has a plan to use us—regardless of what might seem best to us at the time.

I visited with the pastor and his wife and quickly became

involved with the youth group activities. It was something I enjoyed, and it offered great opportunity to be of service. Ardeth too was committed to the youth ministry at the church, and we frequently crossed paths during Sunday night youth activities.

On one particular evening, I was in the parsonage meeting with the pastor's wife planning a Hayrack Ride youth event. As we sat at the dining room table discussing the upcoming outing, the front door opened and in walked Ardeth. She matter-of-factly strode over to the pastor's wife Charlane and gave her a kiss on the cheek exclaiming, "Hi mom!" Up to that point, I had no idea that Ardeth (who led the singing and I met at church every Sunday for the past several weeks) was the pastor's daughter.

***

Ultimately, our courtship advanced quickly. We both worked with the youth and through that interaction, I became enchanted with this lovely young woman who loved the Lord first and foremost. I finally worked up the courage to ask Ardeth for a date. The Milwaukee Opera was a client of Growth Design, and our company frequently had access to tickets. This particular performance was a pre-season 'operetta' composed of a collection of songs from various operas.

Ardeth graciously consented to join me for the evening and off we went. The challenge for most with opera is everything is in a foreign language. Often the characters convey the story line through elaborate backdrops, sets, costuming, singing and acting. Not so with an operetta. There are no costumes; there is no story line—just a blend of songs from numerous productions.

At intermission, I asked Ardeth, "What do you think so far?" With a gallant attempt at cordiality, she replied, "Well, it's interesting." With a quick assessment of how the evening was progressing, I suggested, "Let's go somewhere else." We gratefully headed for Baker's Square for some French Silk pie. But that was the beginning.

The next few months were magical. It was so fun to be 'falling in love.' But I was also hesitant, having been engaged to a girl once before. This time I wanted to be sure Ardeth was the right one. I remember the first time we held hands. It was Saturday, and we were window shopping in a historic suburb of Milwaukee. When it came time to cross the street, as I stepped off the curb, I reached behind me to pull Ardeth safely along side. She clasped my hand and when we reached the other side of the street, she never let go. After all these years, she still hasn't.

Ardeth's strength and unshakeable faith impressed me even back then. One evening we were walking in the neighborhood. As we meandered along the sidewalks, I asked a rhetorical question, "What happens if it doesn't work out between us?" Immediately, Ardeth got around in front of me, placed both hands on my arms, and announced unequivocally, "That is not an option." I thought to myself, this woman is either crazy, or she truly understands the meaning of real commitment.

God works in powerful ways and without a doubt, He has plans for our lives. While we might like some of His plans, others we may not. But ultimately God is sovereign, and He is in control. As a result of this "divine appointment," Ardeth and I began dating in the fall, were engaged on Valentine's Day and were married on Saturday, June 21, 1986.

Prior to that, true to my traditional leanings, I called my then pastor and future father-in-law, Ard Blomberg, asking for time to get together for coffee. We met at the local McDonalds and I said, "Ard, I plan to ask Ardeth to marry me. I'm not asking for your permission, but I would greatly value your blessing." He replied with a smile, "You have them both under one condition, you put God first."

***

Looking back at the time God convicted me to visit Asbury Theological Seminary, He was also convicting Ardeth. That same summer of 1985, while I was wrestling with God about the direction for my life, God was also at work in Ardeth's life.

In June, Ardeth attended Wesleyan Family Camp. The Northern District of the Wesleyan Church maintained a small church camp ground just outside Hillsboro, Wisconsin. Nestled in the rolling fields of alfalfa and corn, Burr Camp was in the heart of dairy country.

Ardeth had been attending Burr Camp since she was a young child as her dad had been a pastor in the Wisconsin District of the Wesleyan Church for over 30 years.

Now in her early twenties, she was back attending a week of Family Camp—a wonderful time of reunion with her family and friends developed from many previous summers of youth camps.

During the evening service in the old tabernacle building, the guest speaker challenged the audience to live their lives fully for God's service and to His glory. Ardeth knew she was a Christian and that Jesus Christ had already paid the price for her salvation. But she also knew that she had not truly made Him Lord of her life. She was still in control—not Him.

At the conclusion of the sermon, the speaker offered an altar call for all those desiring to re-commit their lives to Christ. The audience began singing one last song in closing, and God started speaking directly to Ardeth's heart. During the first verse, Ardeth was convinced that she needed to go forward. She struggled within, and as the audience began singing the second verse, the pull became stronger.

Still reluctant, as the third verse began, Ardeth gave in to the gentle tug of the voice of God and she went forward.

An older woman, Keitha, walked up to the front and knelt beside Ardeth. She prayed with Ardeth as she was now weeping uncontrollably. Keitha asked her, "Why are you crying?" Ardeth answered, "Because I'm afraid."

"Afraid of what," Keitha questioned. "I'm afraid of what He may ask me to do for Him," replied Ardeth. Keitha assured her, "I don't know what God will ask of you. But I do know that whatever it is, He will walk with you through it all."

Ardeth had no inkling of exactly what was in store for her as she committed her life and future family in service to Christ that evening. The Bible never said following Christ would be easy. In fact, it says just the opposite. But Jesus also promised that He would "never leave nor forsake us."

Our challenge is keeping our eyes on Him. I remember the story of a woman from our previous church in Lakeville,

Minnesota, who had a dream about following Christ. She was on the beach, and Jesus walked in front of her. And as they went, she tried harder and harder to place her feet in the exact footprints Jesus had left in advance of her. But the harder she tried to match stride-for-stride His footprints, she noticed she was falling farther and farther behind. Beginning to panic for fear of losing Him, she took her focus off the footprints and focused once again on watching Jesus. Soon she caught-up and was able to stay with Him, as long as she kept her focus on Him, not on the footprints.

✳✳✳

We found ourselves starting married life in Bloomington, Minnesota—each with a new job to begin the following week. Our brief honeymoon was limited to one night at the Midway Holiday Inn in Lacrosse, Wisconsin, because I had accepted an assignment to start on Monday with a client in the Twin Cities. Fortunately, Ardeth had arranged a transfer to the Twin Cities office of the national disability insurance company where she had previously been employed in Milwaukee.

Those first few years of marriage were magical. We rented our first apartment together. We managed to buy our first home in a new neighborhood of Burnsville surrounded by other newly married couples, many of whom we stay in touch with today. And we began our life-long passion for traveling together. Whenever we could manage, we'd take a vacation. Florida was first, followed by a cruise. Those wonderful experiences are what we continued to develop with our kids.

Three years later, in the fall of 1989, shortly before the birth of our first child, Kjrsten, I left Growth Design Corporation after I was recruited to run the finance committee for David Printy—a gubernatorial candidate in Minnesota. At the Republican Endorsing Convention held in Duluth in June of 1990, after seven ballots, Printy didn't win the convention. Politics is a fickle friend—one day I had a steady income, the next day I didn't.

Now what? No job, no immediate prospects. A mortgage at 10.5 percent interest (a good rate for that time) on a starter home and a nine-month-old daughter. I was understandably nervous.

Although I had resigned my position as a consultant with Growth Design to take on the governor's race, I had maintained good relations with the company president to whom I had reported directly. After admitting to myself that an appointment to the governor's staff was obviously not in my future, I was preparing to call my former employer at Growth Design and return to the work I knew and enjoyed— consulting with non-profits for major fundraising campaigns.

As I struggled with the decision, my wife (smart woman) challenged me to consider another option. She asked, "Why don't you go out on your own?" I told Ardeth I wasn't ready, and she retorted, "You're crazy."

In the end, it was her irrefutable logic that prevailed. Ardeth wisely asked, "What is the worst thing that could happen? Try it, and if it doesn't work, you'll be unemployed. Guess what—you're unemployed now!"

As a result of Ardeth's encouragement, in July of 1990 we took the leap of faith, established Renaissance Group, Inc., and God blessed our efforts. We never looked back.

We were humbled in our daily walk to answer the call to strive to be good parents because now the Hoeksemas were a family of four. After the birth of our daughter Kjrsten, my wife Ardeth and I were blessed 22 months later with a son. Continuing in the Scandinavian tradition, we named him Hans. As I mentioned before, living in the suburbs of Minneapolis, Minnesota, afforded us the opportunity to bless our children with unique Scandinavian names.

Now, two years later, my independent consulting business was doing well and Ardeth had been promoted to office manager of Provident Disability Insurance Company, Minneapolis Branch Office. Good news—bad news. We were both swamped.

On one particular Saturday morning, I packed up two-year-old Kjrsten, and Ardeth packed up three-month-old Hans as we each headed out to our respective offices to catch up on work. When we returned home later that day, it was time for a serious family discussion. I emphatically said to Ardeth, "This simply can't continue. It's not fair to the kids, and it's not fair to us. Something has to change."

We carefully weighed our options and decided Ardeth would sacrifice her career to stay at home with our children. It was a very difficult decision. Ardeth had a stable position with benefits. I had potential earning capacity with lots of risk and no benefits. How were we going to survive on one unknown salary? We continue to pray today as we did then, "God, give us the clients you want us to serve and keep us from the ones we shouldn't." And He was, and continues to be, so faithful.

I once had a client ask me, "You don't advertise and you're

not listed in the phone book. How do you get clients?"

"It's all 'word of mouth referrals,'" I replied. I shared with him how we pray and ask God to direct us to the right clients to serve. He asked, "But shouldn't you give Him some help?" I quickly responded, "God doesn't need my help."

***

During this time, we attended a very small Wesleyan Church in Burnsville. We led the only adult Sunday school class, and I filled the pulpit when our pastor was gone. Unfortunately, there was not a children's program for our kids. We felt torn—wanting to leave for a larger church with children's programming but felt like we couldn't leave for the damage it would do to our small struggling church. I knew our tithe was important to the church finances.

I shared my honest concerns with a friend and pastor of another church. His response shook me to the core. "That's awfully arrogant of you," he said. "If God wants that church to prosper, He will make a way—with or without you." I had my answer. I was released, and shortly thereafter, we joined an Evangelical Free Church in another suburb of Minneapolis—Lakeville. Our family was blessed to be part of a church with a strong and growing children's ministry. (Thanks, Julie Anderson.)

By now we had graduated to a larger home closer to our church community in Lakeville. Two healthy, happy kids made for an extremely satisfying home life. Those early years of our young family are exquisite treasures. We watched as our kids learned to swim in the hot tub. "I swimmin dad, I swimmin!" gleefully exclaimed 4-year old Hans. I taught Kjrsten how to ride a bicycle in our driveway. Enjoying from the sidelines as the kids steered their battery-operated hot wheel jeeps—Kjrsten's was Barbie pink and Hans' was GI Joe camouflage. Ardeth and I share wonderful memories from our time in Lakeville.

✳✳✳

But my restless spirit kept us moving farther from the city. In 1996, we purchased 40 acres in rural Northfield, Minnesota. Our plan was to build our own home in the country. Recognizing the magnitude of the undertaking, I wanted to be as close to the project as possible. Accordingly, we looked around for a mobile home to move onto the property where we could live while we built our dream home. The search was a challenge. Between Rice County zoning restrictions that dictated the size of mobile homes and the lack of inventory, our ultimate selection left a lot to be desired. We eventually purchased a 16' x 70' three bedroom mobile home that had been repossessed by the bank.

The previous owners had been less than kind to our new home. We moved the trailer to our building site and proceeded to tear out all the carpeting. The siding was rotting and one window had to be completely removed. We bought the most inexpensive pre-backed carpet we could find and re-carpeted most of the interior. My new neighbor, Mike Schlossin, was a friend from church, and we had been together on missions trips to Mexico. He was also a stucco man. Mike came over and we tar-papered and lathed the trailer in anticipation of ultimately stuccoing a mobile home. While it didn't look very attractive, it was weatherproof—a vital necessity for surviving Minnesota winters.

That first winter was an incredible challenge. There was no garage, and Minnesosta weather piled nearly six feet of snow on us that year. It was also bitterly cold which didn't suit the above-ground mobile home with no basement to protect the pipes. If we didn't constantly keep the cabinet doors in the kitchen open, the pipes froze.

We later discovered that we hadn't put down enough rock and gravel for a temporary driveway and paid the price when the spring thaw came. The ruts in the drive were nearly a foot deep and only our four-wheel-drive Blazer could navigate them—on select days.

At the time, people thought we were out of our minds, but some of our best memories are from that old and tired mobile home. I still recall digging snow forts with the kids. We had no dishwasher and would wash and dry our dishes together as family. This is also where we began the life lessons we hoped would serve our children well as adults. The first lesson was introducing them to hard work.

We built a stick barn and began raising cattle. The kids bought three calves from a local farmer and were responsible for chores every day. We would go into town and buy feed in 50 pound bags. We watched as Hans and Kjrsten learned to work together by going out to the barn and manhandling those bags into garbage cans. This made it easier in the morning for them to scoop out the appropriate amount of feed for the calves before heading off to catch the school bus.

Living on the farm provided numerous opportunities for

teachable moments. One of the best was the necessity to feed the livestock (horses, cows, chickens) regardless of the weather or the prevailing mood. Early every morning, Hans and Kjrsten would faithfully and without complaining, accomplish their assigned tasks. And in return, they were rewarded when it came time to sell the fattened cattle. They quickly learned the value of hard work and its accompanying rewards.

Learning to handle money at an early age also afforded the kids the opportunity to learn that all we have been given is entrusted by God. Our responsibility is to be a good steward with His resources.

For Hans and Kjrsten that lesson began with tithing back 10 percent of all their cattle profits to the church.

We also raised chickens (some for fryers and others for laying eggs), and the kids were assigned to gather the eggs. Hans would complain frequently about reaching under the noisily clucking hens who would peck at his hand as he tried to collect their eggs.

✳✳✳

Setting up a hobby farm takes a lot of work. One of my first priorities was to purchase a vintage tractor. So late in December, Kjrsten and I went to a farm auction in search of a tractor. We didn't find what I was looking for, but Kjrsten found something precious to her just the same. It was so cold that day that Kjrsten was close to tears. I felt so badly for her that when we came across a cardboard box full of puppies with a sign 'free to a good home,' I relented. Kjrsten chose the runt of the litter, a beautiful little female with the coloring of a German shepherd. With the puppy tucked deep inside her winter coat, all of a sudden Kjrsten wasn't feeling quite so cold.

When we arrived back at our home-on-wheels, Ardeth was beside herself. We already had two kittens that Kjrsten had adopted, and we now had added a puppy to the menagerie. Kjrsten named her Sugar. Suddenly, the mobile home was feeling a little cramped.

It took us 18 months to complete construction of our home. It was a beauty. We perched the house on a hill that had sweeping vistas to the west. A huge front porch with cedar plank siding and log posts created the comfort and rustic feel we enjoyed so much. I added a log loft for my in-home office. Over time we planted a huge garden and canned a wide-variety of foods—stewed tomatoes, sweet corn, homemade salsa, green beans, peas, carrots, potatoes and more.

I continued to travel as much as ever and that created a unique set of challenges. We had 50 fryers that year and as it so happened, I was on the road when the time came to take the chickens to the butcher who accepted chickens on select days—and by 5:30 a.m. only. As a result, it was left to Ardeth to handle the task. She faithfully set her alarm for 3:30 am in order to bag the birds and meet the butcher's deadline. As Ardeth came out of our bedroom that morning, there sat Kjrsten. "What are you doing up?" asked Ardeth. "I figured you could use the help," said a sleepy nine-year-old Kjrsten.

So, the two of them set off to round up the chickens. When they got to the barn, the dilemma of how to transport the birds became obvious. Ultimately, they settled on stuffing the birds into feed sacks, tying off the ends and throwing the wiggling bags into the back of the pickup. Another mission accomplished. Kjrsten went back to bed, and Ardeth headed off to the butcher.

For our growing dog and cats, we often left pet food outside. Not only did our pets appreciate the gesture so did the local variety of wildlife. This particular morning there was a skunk in our garage. He had wandered in and made his way down the stairs to the basement entrance in the garage and was now confused as how to climb back up the stairs and extricate himself from his new predicament.

I was in a hurry to catch my flight but wanted to be helpful as well. I went back inside and retrieved my 12 gauge shotgun and returned to the garage. Peering over the top of the four foot safety wall surrounding the access to the basement stairs, I hoisted the gun over the top, took a quick glance to confirm my aim, pulled my head back to avoid any ricocheting pellets, and fired. I hit the skunk but not as strategically as I had envisioned. In fact, skunk stink was now oozing from the dead carcass sitting at the bottom of the stairs leading to our basement. I, on the other hand, had a plane to catch.

Ardeth, a real team player, was left to deal with the incredible stench that only a ruptured skunk can exude. Left with no choice but to deal with the mess by herself, she gagged and coughed her way through the cleanup job. She was (and still is) quite the trooper.

During these years, Ardeth and I continued our interest and service to the youth in our church. When junior high Sunday school teachers were in short supply, we volunteered. And, instead of losing track of the youth we taught, we chose to stay with them as their Sunday school teachers while they advanced through high school. We spent several years with those youth who still today remain our friends on facebook.

Investing in our family was a high priority for us. Because of my extensive travel for work, I accumulated more than one million Frequent Flyer miles that we routinely converted into free tickets for family vacations. We made a deal with Hans and Kjrsten that as long as they maintained good grades we would allow them to miss school for family trips. Consequently, we were blessed to have traveled around the world with our children even at their young ages.

Both Hans and Kjrsten were certified Open Water scuba divers. On one of our vacations, I thought it would be a great idea to earn certification while on the cruise. It meant sacrificing half of each day on the cruise for classroom work, pool work or check-out dives.

Hans and Kjrsten agreed to this plan, and I was ecstatic thinking this was an activity we could share together for years to come. After the first three days of classes, Hans who was 12 at the time, decided only to complete the Junior Diver certification and have the remaining three days of the cruise for pure recreation. Kjrsten finished the entire course with me. Only later did I learn from Ardeth that Kjrsten really wasn't all that excited about learning to dive, but she didn't want to hurt her Dad's feelings. A few months later while in Cozumel, Hans completed his diving certification, and all three of us enjoyed drift-diving in Mexico together.

Some of our trips were focused on relaxation and others Ardeth termed as "educational trips." With a major in history in college, I had managed to pass some of that love for history on to our children. Wherever we traveled, we always looked for the historical learning opportunities that could be coupled with the excursion. Visiting New Orleans, we stopped at the Civil War battlefield in Vicksburg, Mississippi. In Georgia, we saw Stone Mountain and toured the POW Museum at Andersonville. Touring France, we devoted three days to exploring the beaches of the D-Day invasion at Normandy.

We even took time to stop at little country cemeteries in the Midwest. We found head stones with the unique war insignias indicating military service in each of the major wars. After one such impromptu visit, I remember Hans commenting, "I thought this was going to be boring, but it turned out to be fun."

✳✳✳

But investing in our children's lives went far deeper than family vacations. Ardeth and I believed that raising children was very much a proactive enterprise that required spending time with our children. Dr. John Trent and Gary Smalley co-authored a book several years ago entitled *The Blessing* that confirms our thoughts on raising children. They make a convincing case for how important it is for us to pass 'the blessing' on to our children. It represents our unconditional gift of love and acceptance that is crucial for children as they grow and develop.

I'll never forget the advice of one of my peers at Growth Design. Dan Thurmer is a former Lutheran pastor as well as a good friend and great mentor for whom I have utmost respect.

Dan taught me one of my greatest lessons when he told me, "I used to believe the greatest calling any of us can have is to the pastorate. I don't believe that anymore. The greatest calling is to be a good parent."

A LONG GOODBYE

A fitting conclusion to our story seemed appropriate when I re-discovered a letter Ardeth had written to Kjrsten two months after her death.

November 17, 2004
Dear Kjrsten:

Oh, Baby—Do I ever miss you! There are so many things I want to share with you each and every day. And the memories seem to hit me at the strangest times. I smile and then the loss smothers me into sadness. I keep telling myself to hang on; there are dreams around the corner yet to experience. Dreams with Dad and Hans; future joy to embrace. So I make a choice to hold on for those promises of tomorrows. I must tell you it is so hard because as soon as I look forward to tomorrow I realize you won't be there to laugh, smile, cry or hold onto. That is so painful.

People keep telling me how strong I am or how strong Dad

is. We talk about this and say, "What are our choices?" We can't quit; we aren't quitters and we never raised any quitters, in our children. You would be the first to jump in and say, "Hey, you never raised me that way—you can't stop now—think of the tomorrows with all the blessings you told me about as I was growing up!"

I watch children often, younger ones, and remember how determined you were to experience everything. Your laughter at yourself and others was always infectious. I really miss the laughter, the deep, shaking your body laughter. You could incite a riot of laughter.

✳✳✳

I was remembering how frightened you were after you were thrown from the horse. You had the wind knocked out of you. You were only 9. Boy, did you cry. You refused to get on that horse again. You said horses frightened you. In the fall, we purchased a 29 year old mare named Buffy, and you fell in love all over again. We assured you she wouldn't run off with you, and you just smiled. You had hope of enjoying horses again.

I remember watching out the window on a winter day when it was lightly snowing. You took a treat out to Buffy. I watched as you took a plastic garbage can and turned it upside down, put it right up next to her and got on. You stretched out as far as you could and laid your head on her neck. You stayed that way for at least 15 minutes, just rubbing her neck and side. Then, it was time to move. You jumped off and then got back on. I watched you do this for about another 15 minutes. You hugged her and turned to the house. You had such a big smile on your face, and you bounced all the way to the house.

As soon as you hit the door, you had to start telling me of your adventure, and of Buffy and you making friends. I miss your adventures so very much.

My mind trips from dates and times with no rhyme or reason. In one memory you are young and another you are older. I remember the very first time you actually got to drive the old pick-up truck by yourself. Dad needed help in the field, picking up square hay bales. Dad looked at you and wondered. When he offered you the opportunity, according to Dad, you jumped at the chance to drive and help your Dad.

How you loved working with your Dad! He misses your willingness to work beside him with your smile and constant conversation. Dad said you picked driving up quickly. I remember coming home while you were driving. You had the bench seat pulled up as far as it could go. You couldn't see over the dash if you sat back, so you had yourself pulled up by your arms as close to the steering wheel as possible. It couldn't have been the easiest position, but the smile on your face was brilliant. Dad would tap the truck and you would pull ahead to the next bale. You would stop, look over your shoulder and wait for the next tap. You were both so excited about this new experience. I think you were only 8 years old. Even when you were only 6 and 7 you would follow Dad out to do an odd job with him. You thrived on working and being with Dad.

I remember one night we had company—about 8 people. You and Hans weren't interested in visiting, only being 7 and 9 years old.

After dinner, you grabbed Hans (or Hansy as you called

him), and a book and settled on the couch. I remember listening and smiling how you are reading the story and adding bits and pieces to make it more exciting. You explained the "plot" of the story, and then the laughter came quickly as he asked questions and made comments. You got up and went to get another one for another round.

I remember one of the women commenting on how impressed she was that even at your age, you were reading out loud to another child. You had such a large heart and care for children, even being a child yourself. Plus you had a heart for Hans, always encouraging him when he was little.

✳✳✳

This brings me to current memories; you used to get so frustrated with him for his "immaturity," and I would laugh and say "give him time." Just love him, I would say. I laughed and said how in a few years he will be taller than you, stronger and ready to face the world with his maturity. You would laugh, shake your head—I think wondering if it was ever going to happen. How I wish you could see what a man he will be some day.

Even in your frustration, you encouraged Hans. Remember the day this fall when he came home hurt because some boys were picking on him at lunch, pushing him around by telling him where he could sit. You told him to be courageous and stand up for himself. You told him to just say "no" when they tell you to move. "Keep it short and sweet," you said with a smile. Then you proceeded to tell him if that didn't work to let you know. You had some friends who would be willing to beat them up if they kept picking on your "little brother." I asked why would your "friends" be willing to beat up someone for you. You smiled that cocky smile, the one that was laughing and had secrets too, and said, "Because they truly love me, Mom." I shook my head and just laughed. You shrugged your shoulders, and we all laughed together. Do I ever miss our laughing together.

Remember when Dad traveled so much when we lived in Minnesota? We had a load of chickens to go to butcher. I had to get up at 3:30 am to load them up and get them to the locker by 5:30 am and be back to get you and Hans on the bus by 7 am. You guys were so good. You always got up to alarm clocks since you were in the 1st grade (of course Hans wasn't in school and usually slept through it). I told both you guys what I was doing so you wouldn't worry when you got up. I had my phone with me and if you needed me, you could call. When I opened my bedroom door at 3:30 am, what met my eyes, but a sleepy eyed, smiling midget ready to be my helper. I asked why you were up and you gave me that look of love, replying, "I thought you might need some help." You were in the 3rd grade, only nine years old. We walked out to the barn together and after several attempts to get the truck loaded with 50 chickens—success! I told you several times after, I couldn't have done it without your help. This was so you, to make an effort above and beyond. You went back to bed, saying, "I love you." The chickens and I went to the locker. When I returned at 7am, you were up, showered and ready for the bus. You made sure Hans was ready to go too. Did I ever thank you for being such a great sister to Hans? I hope I did!

Again, back to recent history, when Dad took off at 3 am in early September for a fishing trip. I kissed your Daddy goodbye and rolled over to go back to sleep. Dad talked with me later to say you were waiting for him outside our bedroom door to let him know you loved him and send him off. Oh my baby—how we miss you!

Track was always a sport you suffered through with a smile and sigh. You really didn't like running that much, partly because you felt you were not very fast. Yet, you made the effort, even running at home in an effort to improve yourself. I remember the race when you had the chance to break the ribbon. It was the 400, and you pushed yourself. When you crossed the line to break the tape, your smile was wide and brilliant. You jumped up and down and yelled, "I broke it!" You ran over to me laughing and dancing so excited. You kept saying, "I broke it! I broke it!" Finally after taking a breath, you gave me that cocky grin and admitted "it was the third heat (the slowest in the whole event), but I broke the tape." You laughed and danced some more. It was like you were the fastest runner of the day, and your success overshadowed everything else.

This is how I imagine you lived every aspect of your life, understanding your limitations, yet rejoicing in "doing your very best, with your greatest effort." You were truly a gifted young woman, not in your achievements in the world, but in your spirit and attitude of what is most important—the things on the inside matter—the heart!

I truly feel an emptiness so often throughout each day knowing you will not greet me with an attitude of excitement for what happened throughout your day. You never expected perfect, untroubled days, but you knew you could find joy somewhere in the hours and minutes that passed. There was not a single event or person who didn't get your attention, all these moments you shared with laughter, a shake of the head in disappointment or sometime even in tears.

✳✳✳

Your convictions were amazing, wrong was wrong, and yet you had compassion for others. Remember after the Baxter track meet in 8th grade, we went to dinner at O'Kelly's, just you and me (I honestly don't know where Dad and Hans were). While eating, you regaled the day and meet, your disappointments and successes. You then mentioned a girl in your class (a new girl in school you were reluctant to spend any time with because of her choices) was attempting to sell pot to your friends. You were always so honest with your Dad and me. We talked about the choices both good and bad each of us can make. I asked you if you were willing to tell, you just smiled sadly and said, "I don't want to be called a snitch." But with everyone knowing, you felt sure someone of importance would find out. We continued to eat. I feel I made the right choice, honey. I notified the school and asked them to do their best to keep your name out of the picture. However, if they couldn't, I would understand.

They did a great job of protecting you and assuring me they would. The next day, the girl was arrested for possession and selling. You came home from school with this grin, crinkling eyes and said "Mom, she was arrested, even with handcuffs." You paused a moment and said, "Someone must have told, I'm glad they did." You were so honest, even when it could have meant trouble for yourself. Thank you for being honest.

This year you had some difficult courses. You were worried, concerned but not discouraged. Positive you could do your best. To do your best was just par for your course in life. In Current Events you had to write a paper on the Arab–Israeli conflict. I remember you discussing it with Dad in detail. You asked some questions and used some resources, as required. What impressed me most was you actually used the Bible to point out the beginning of the Arab–Israeli conflict. You started at the very beginning with Abraham and his sons, Isaac and Ishmael. You got a good grade, but most impressive to me was your willingness to step out in your belief that the Bible was an authority. How many 14-year-old girls or boys would put it down for their teachers to read, much less discuss with their friends. Wow—you impressed me so much with your courage. I'm not sure when you got the paper back, but Dad and I finally looked at it the week after the funeral. Sometimes it is so hard to look at what you accomplished because we think of "what she would have been or accomplished."

Animal Science was a class you enjoyed this year. Do you realize you were only in school less than four weeks? Several days after the accident I found poster board, copies of animals' internal organs, markers and such. You were assigned to a group (of two boys), and it concerned you. You didn't feel your group was going to do very well since the rest of your group wasn't doing anything. You were a leader though. I remember the week before you decided you were going to hand out assignments. You gave a boy a project to look up a particular animal. Several days after you asked him what he had found. He told you he hadn't had time. You said to him, "Would you please have it by Friday?" He rode away on his bike, and you heard him mumble, "Yeah, I will get right on it—not." You came home in tears, not sure how to handle this. We told you to talk to your teacher, and tell him of your concerns. The next day you shared your concerns with the instructor. He assured you not to worry, he would take into account the situation. Just do your best, he encouraged. The assignment was due Friday, September 17th. On Wednesday, you were in tears again. Dad and I sat down with you, and we talked about possibilities and how to make a "success" of what appeared to be an "unsuccessful" situation. We explained that no matter what the grade reflects, you know, the instructor knows and we know that you did your best. After the discussion, you made a "to do list" and assigned responsibility. My responsibility was to get markers, poster board and enlarged copies of the animal. By the end of the night, you were excited about the possibilities and your potential success.

In talking with Deb Dillon, she mentioned what you were talking about before the accident. You were looking forward to spending Thursday night, September 16th, working on the project. You explained the suggestions Dad had given you about the presentation. You were excited and laughing about how you were going to actually do it. How I wish we could have worked on that project together. I miss working with you and encouraging you with your homework.

As I sit here writing this letter, more memories get tossed about. Laughter, tears, loving times, times of anticipation and excitement for life. I do miss you every day. My heart hurts almost physically. Do you know there are days at work, I actually just lay my head down on my desk and weep? You were my very best girlfriend. You were the one I would do everything "feminine" with. Do you know the difficulty I have in going to Kohl's or Target without crying? It is very hard. I think that part of my life is over. No more excitement about boys, hair, jewelry, clothes and shoes. Painting nails and getting the hair done just don't work with Dad or Hans.

Remember last year in October how we went to get a pedicure together. We sat side by side talking and softly laughing about the experience. I know someday I will probably have it done again, but it won't be the same. I will think of the first time and miss you all over again. I do think that is the very hardest thing for me. Never doing those "Mother/Daughter" things together. You gave me such great joy by being a lovely young woman and wanting, yes, actually wanting to do those things with me. Thank you so very much for those precious memories. How I wish we could have made so many more. I really wanted to share these experiences with you and maybe your daughter some day. The possibilities are endless. You would have made an awesome mother.

Christmas last year was a revelation to so many in the family. Everyone came out to our house, numbering a total of 22. The newest member of the family and only great grandchild, Cloey, was only two years old at the time. Remember during the quiet time, where Grandpa Hoeksema read the Christmas Story and then went on to tell some personal insights he had the last year. Cloey was busy and making some "child" sounds. You got up and went to her. You smiled and kept her busy, talking with her and playing right where she was quietly. Who is going to entertain Cloey this year?

Actually, in my mind I look forward to it. Imagine a parent carrying on a torch of a child, what an awesome thing. It always amazed me to see of all the grandchildren there, six of them being girls and all older than you—the oldest being in college, then two seniors, a junior and a freshman. Yet, you were the one with the heart to care for Cloey, not because you were immature, but because you weren't.

There is so much more I could say or write and my heart could feel. I think I have written enough for now. Sometime I think if I could go back and just relive the last 14 years over and over again I would. However, I don't get to choose in this life, do I? I love you so very much, it is sometimes so hard to verbally describe what I feel. I miss you so much and it hurts, even physically sometimes. Thank you, Kjrsten, for being so much more than any parent or friend could even imagine.

Love,
Mom

CHAPTER NOTES

Grateful acknowlegment is made to the authors and publishers for the use of the following material. Every effort has been made to credit original sources and request permission to quote. If notified, the author, will be pleased to rectify any omission in future editions.

Introduction
1. Joni Eareckson Tada, *The God I Love*, Zondervan, 2003.

Chapter Two: Sunshine and Shadow
1. Robert Lewis, *Raising a Modern Day Knight*, Tyndale House, 2007.

Chapter Five: Long Days Journey Into Night
1. Matt Redman, vocal performance of *Blessed Be Your Name*, written by Beth and Matt Redman on Where Angels Fear to tread, released 2002, Survivor Records, compact disc

Chapter Six: Letting Go
1. A Ragamuffin Band, vocal performance of *My Redeemer*, written by Rich Mullins and Mitch McVicker on Jesus Record, released 1998, Myrrh label, compact disc
2. Steven Curtis Chapman, vocal performance of *Fingerprints of God*, written by Steven Curtis Chapman and Geoff Moore on Speechless, released 1999, Sparrow Records, compact disc

3. Twila Paris, vocal performance of *The Warrior is a Child*, written by Gary Valenciano on Looking Up, released 2006, Sony Special Product compact disc

Chapter Seven: Heaven's Gate
1. Mercy Me, vocal performance of *I Can Only Imagine*, written by Bart Millard on Word of God Speak, released 2001, INO/Curb, compact disc
2. Charles Swindoll, *Job—A man of heroic endurance*, Thomas Nelson Inc., 2004 (dedication, 1,3,4,12)
3. Collin Raye, vocal performance of *Love Me*, written by Skip Ewing and Max T. Barnes, on All I can Be released 1991, Epic, compact disc

Chapter Eight: The God of All Comfort
1. *Standing on Holy Ground* arranged by Geron Davis, 1983, Meadowgreen Music.

Chapter Nine: Light Shining in the Darkness
1. Eugene Peterson, Introduction to Job, from *The Message*, Colorado Springs, CO: Nav Press, 2002 (839).

Chapter Ten: Mercies in Disguise
1. Bruce Wilkinson with David Kopp, *A life God rewards for teens*, Multnomah Publishers, 2002.
2. Dr. John Trent and Gary Smalley, *The Blessing*, Thomas Nelson, 1986.